Computers & The Internet Made Simple

Mark Meakings

www.computertrainingexpert.co.uk

Published by Gotham New Media Ltd
PO Box 23, Bexhill on Sea TN39 4ZU, England
Email: info@computertrainingexpert.co.uk
Web: www.computertrainingexpert.co.uk

This book is copyright. Enquiries should be addressed
to the author c/o the publishers.

© Mark Meakings 2009.
The right of Mark Meakings to be identified as the author of this work
has been asserted in accordance with the Copyright, Designs and Patent Act 1988.

ISBN:978-0-9559521-3-5
All Rights reserved. No part of this publication may be reproduced, stored in a retrieval
system or transmitted, in any form or by any means, electronic, mechanical, photocopying,
recording or otherwise without the prior written permission of the author and publisher.
This book is sold subject to the condition that it shall not by way of trade or otherwise
be lent, re-sold, hired out or otherwise circulated without the publisher's prior consent
in any form of binding or cover other than that in which it is published.

"Windows" is a trademark of Microsoft Corporation. "Mac" is a trademark of Apple Inc.
"KAZ" is a trademark of Gotham New Media. All other trademarks are acknowledged.

A catalogue record for this book is available from the British Library.

Printed and bound in Great Britain

Copies are available at special rates for bulk orders.
Contact the sales development team on 01424 842570 for more information.

Disclaimer

Gotham New Media Ltd are providing this written material on an 'as is' basis and make no
(and expressly disclaim all) representations or warranties of any kind with respect to this
written material or its contents including, without limitation, advice and recommendations,
warranties or merchantability and fitness for a particular purpose. The information is
given for entertainment purposes only. The author or the publisher will not be liable for
damages arising out of or in connection with the use of this written material. This is a
comprehensive limitation of liability that applies to all damages of any kind, including
(without limitation) compensatory, direct, indirect or consequential damages, loss of
data, income or profit, loss of or damage to property and claims of third parties.

Dedication

This book is the culmination of many hours of hard work and the loyal support of the people who have encouraged me to help others learn how to use technology to change their lives.

Chris, my wife, without whose continual support and encouragement this book would never have been possible. Steve Tyrrell who has amazing abilities to manage our business so effectively and calmly, thus giving me the room to write. Veronica Lovett, who keeps me organised. Professor Marc Eisenstadt, one of the brightest men I know who has just retired as Chief Scientist at the Open University and who has inspired me. To Jenny Tyrrell for her skill and patience in editing this book and to all the positive and encouraging people who have strengthened me in my personal journey of life.

A Reader's Comment...

"This book is a must for anyone wanting to get the most out of their computer. Comprehensive information, with links to lots more information, given in non-techy language that is easy to understand. So often we touch the surface of the wonderful new technology out there (digital cameras, mobiles, MP3s, even microwaves!). Reading this book makes you realise how much we are missing, and how relatively simply we can access so much. So don't be left behind or frightened by the new techy revolution, help has finally arrived..." **Pauline Oakley**

Introduction

I believe to be effective, learning should be concise and directed at what you need to know, when you need to know it. As an example, when I first looked at the methods that were being used to teach people to type correctly I discovered to my dismay that I needed to work through dozens of exercises that took hours of boring keyboard drills. So it's no wonder when I looked around I didn't see many people "touch typing"!

My solution to that problem was to create a new simple method to teach people to touch type the a-z keys. Then to provide additional training to enable people to improve their typing skills and to learn more as and when they wanted to.

Consequently the "KAZ" (short for Keyboard A to Z) typing tutor reduced learning times to an average of just 90 minutes! KAZ has made learning so easy that organisations like the Open University and Learndirect have provided it to hundreds of thousands of learners. If you are interested in how this is done, visit my website www.computertrainingexpert.co.uk where you can find details of this and other accelerated learning products I have created to help people use computers.

Having developed more than 30 computer courses used by tens of thousands of people, one thing has become clear. Although computer use is widespread, people's skills and knowledge using them varies enormously. The difficulty in writing a book on this subject is trying to make a "one size fits all" solution, which is not ideal. So I have designed this book for a complete beginner to read through, and organised it so that people with more experience can dip in and out of relevant chapters to fill in gaps in their knowledge and understanding.

No matter what level of computer experience you have, you will find valuable and useful information to help you get the most productivity and enjoyment from using your computer.

If you would like to learn more about using software like Windows Vista, Microsoft Word, Excel, Internet Explorer and Outlook Email, I have produced a companion "Learn Microsoft Office and Vista in 90 Minutes" CD ROM. Simply install and run this on your computer. You will see a menu on your screen of programs to learn how to use, plus a series of 3 to 5 minutes training clips that take you step by step through using the programs. These are to dip in and out of whenever you want. You can find details of this CD ROM at www.computertrainingexpert.co.uk.

About The Author

Mark Meakings loves to create quicker and easier ways for people to learn. This started when he became frustrated and quit an evening class on sailing that took 6 weeks of boring lessons to deliver what could easily be understood in one! Since then he has gone on to work at the forefront of accelerated learning.

Mark has created dozens of computer training courses, software products and books that have been used by millions of learners world-wide. These include children at school from 6 to adult, families, seniors at home and employees of global businesses and governments.

He has made many TV appearances with his products and has consulted on intellectual property rights, licensing and marketing with many clients, including the Open University.

Having left school with no educational qualifications, no job and no money, he created his first business in the recruitment industry from scratch aged just 23. He went on to create and build businesses in recruitment, training, computers, games software, retail, franchising, e-commerce and e-learning. He founded and was Principal of a national college that trained 18,000 people a year in computer and career subjects using his courses.

Mark uses computers to generate passive income streams that enable him to work as little as 4 hours a week on his main business. He believes people are missing out on new ways to live, work and retire using computers and he teaches these specialist skills to people of all abilities who want to make life changes.

If you are ready to challenge your assumptions about the steps you must take to learn about computers and the Internet and to put them to life-changing uses, you'll be glad you met Mark! You can sign up for Mark's free newsletter at www.markmeakings.com.

Table Of Contents

Dedication — I
Introduction — II
About The Author — III

Preface — 9

Chapter 1 - 20 Ways To Use Computers That Could Change Your Life — 11

    Writing — 12
    Calendar — 12
    Managing personal finances — 12
    Online banking — 12
    Digital photos — 13
    Ancestry — 13
    Video — 13
    Music — 14
    Audio books — 14
    Podcasts — 14
    Video podcasts — 14
    TV — 15
    Computer to TV — 15
    Games — 16
    Email — 16
    Telephone — 16
    Dating — 17
    Internet surfing — 17
    Learning — 17
    Making money on the Internet — 18
    Conclusion — 18

Chapter 2 - How To Choose The Right Computer
            And Get Off On The Right Foot   19

    Choosing a Computer   20
    Windows PC or Apple Mac   20
    Windows PC   21
    Why choose a Windows PC?   22
    Apple Mac   22
    Why choose an Apple Mac?   23
    Conclusion   23
    Alternative Operating Systems For PC's   23
    What Computer "Hardware" To Buy   23
    The Computer Box And Brain   24
    Motherboard   24
    Central Processing Unit (CPU)   24
    USB Connections   25
    Firewire Connections   25
    Bluetooth Connections   26
    Memory - RAM   26
    Cache Memory   27
    CD/DVD Drive   27
    Hard Disk   28
    The Computer Screen   28
    Dual Screens   29
    Modem   29
    The Printer   30
    Inkjet Printer   30
    Laser Printer   30
    Laptop vs. Desktop Computers   31
    WIFI (Wireless Network)   32
    Wireless Hotspots   34
    WIMAX   35
    Upgrading Or Replacing Your Computer?   35
    Improving Your Current Computer   36
    Defragment Your Hard Disk   36
    Increase Your Hard Disk Capacity   36

Table Of Contents

Increase Internal Memory (RAM)	36
Fix-it Utilities	37
Upgrading To A New Computer	37
Copying Data From Old To New Computers	38
Going Green	38
On A Windows PC	38
On A Mac Computer	39
Recycling	39

Chapter 3 - How To Choose And The Best Way To Buy Your Software Programs   41

So What Is A "Software Program"?	42
How To Buy Your Software Programs	43
Buy The CD ROM From Your Local Computer Shop	44
Buy The CD ROM From A Website Shop	44
Download It Over The Internet	44
Use It Immediately Online	45
What's Best For You	45
What Software Do You Want?	46
Office Suite	47
Word Processor	47
Spreadsheet	48
Graphics	48
Digital Photos	48
Conclusion	48
Basic Software For The Internet	48
Web Browser	49
Email Client	49
Digital Music	49
Freeware And Shareware Programs	49

Chapter 4 - Getting Started Using Your Computer   51

The Desktop	52
Desktop Wallpaper	53

Screensaver	54
Running Software Programs	55
Turning The Computer Off	55

Chapter 5 - How To Organise Your Computer, Work With And Protect Your Files — 57

Creating Folders	58
How To Create A New Folder On The PC	59
How To Create A New Folder On The Apple Mac	60
Creating Shortcuts	60
Deleting Files	63
Permanently Deleting Files From Your Computer	64
Recovering Old Files	65
Finding Files	66
Safeguarding Your Files And Data	67
Backing Up Your Programs	69
What To Do When It All Goes Wrong	70
Uninstalling Programs	71
Stickies	73

Chapter 6 - Discover What The Internet Is, How To Get On It, Protect Your Computer And Have Some Fun — 75

How The Internet Works	76
What Is A Website?	76
What Is A Web Page?	76
What The Internet Looks Like	77
Getting On The Internet	80
Mobile Broadband	81
Email	81
Internet Security	82
Anti Virus Software	84
Firewall	84
Wifi	85

Table Of Contents

    Passwords   85
    Conclusion   87

Chapter 7 - Learn The Basics Of Word Processing Spreadsheets And Other Software Programs Quickly   89

    Using Your Computer (Without The Internet)   90
    Microsoft Word Basics   90
    Starting Word   90
    Using Word   92
    Create A Document   93
    Save And print   96
    Close Word   98
    Spreadsheets   98
    Starting Excel   99
    Using Excel   100
    Using Photo Software   106
    Photo Software   111
    Scanning Old Photos   112
    Managing Your Pictures   112
    Video   112
    Conclusion   115

Chapter 8 - Discover How To Surf The Internet, Enjoy Safe Shopping, Meet Family And Friends Online, Email And More   118

    Getting Connected To The Internet   118
    Everyday Internet Use   120
    Using An Internet Browser Program   120
    History   122
    Cache   122
    Bookmarks or Favourites   123
    Home Page   124
    Print A Web Page   126

Save A Web Page	126
Email To A Friend	126
Searching On The Internet	126
Shopping Online	128
Safe Shopping	129
EBay	130
Amazon	131
Comparison Shopping	131
Music	132
Social Networking	135
Virtual Life	135
Discussion Forums	137
Blog	139
Dating	140
Your Own Domain	141
Video Websites	142
The View From Space	142
Freephone	142
Video Phone	143
Autopilot News And Information	143
Email On The Internet	143
Typical Internet Email	146
Typical ISP Email	146
Conclusion	149

Table Of Contents

Just imagine being able to see and talk to distant relatives and friends all over the world on your computer for free; being able to play and store all your photos and music; being able to shop without leaving home; being able to find the answer to any question; being able to find love and yes, even make money on the Internet by making your computer work for you while you sleep!

These and many, many other life-enhancing opportunities are waiting for you whatever your age, whether you have used a computer before, or whether you have a computer but don't understand how to make the most of it.

I talk with people all the time who have shunned computers altogether. They will often say "I can't see the benefit" or "I could never get to grips with them" or "I'm too old". Sometimes these people can be very negative, but it's their fear of computers, not wanting to look a fool and having no knowledge or confidence to use them that colours their view.

Being "too old" or set in your ways is just in the mind. All you need to do is change your thinking and start enjoying! Some of my most successful students have been 50, 60, and 70 plus. My father-in-law Harry jumped in at the deep end with no previous knowledge or experience. Within a year, he mastered his computer and wrote his autobiography. He buys and sells at Internet auctions, does research and development on the Internet and a whole lot more. The computer has added another dimension to his life. Not bad at 90!

It's small wonder that many of us are put off when looking for a computer. The industry seems to do its best to shroud everything with meaningless jargon and gobbledygook. I've just gone onto the Internet to look for a computer to buy and this is a typical example of what I found:

Base
Intel® Core™ 2 Duo E8400 processor (3.00GHz, 1333MHz, 6MB cache)
Microsoft Operating System
Genuine Windows Vista® Home Premium – English
Monitor
22" Black Wide Flat Panel (E228WFP) – UK/Irish
Video Card
256MB ATI® Radeon™ HD 2400 XT graphics card
Memory
3072MB 667MHz Dual Channel DDR2 SDRAM [2x1024+2x512]
Hard Drive
640GB (2x320GB) 7200rpm SATA Hard Drive – Dual HDD Config
Optical Devices
DVD +/- RW Drive (read/write CD & DVD)

Confused? Don't worry. This book will guide you through the maze in simple-to-understand, layman's language. However, you can see why it's no surprise that many people are put off buying a computer in the first place.

The good news is you don't need a degree, nor do you need to know the computers internal organs. It doesn't matter what age you are. Whether you are studying, working or one of the increasing number of "baby boomers" or retirees struggling to get to grips with computers, your digital life awaits and can open up new horizons and opportunities for you that you can't yet imagine.

As well as the army of people who have yet to get going, there are an equal number who have jumped in but who struggle to understand and get the most from their computers. It's a bit like buying a Porsche and never experiencing the joy of driving it beyond second gear! You know it will go faster, but for the life of you, you don't know how.

I was having a coffee with a friend recently and the conversation got around to someone who had lost most of the work stored on his computer when a virus had infected it over the Internet. This was devastating as he had no computer backup copies of his work. Luckily, most of his crucial work had been printed on paper and he was able to recover it (after days of re-typing it into a computer!). Others are not so fortunate and some even lose their businesses.

Now I assumed my friend was pretty "computer savvy". After all, she used email all the time, typed and printed her work and enjoyed "surfing" the Internet. However, when I asked her what she knew about the dangers of using a computer and how to protect herself, it turns out she was running exactly the same risks everyday that the person who lost it all was!

We talked some more and, while I was able to praise her for the way she was using her computer, it turned out she had no idea how they work. She didn't know how to get the best from them or what amazing and life changing opportunities they could open up for her beyond the limited use she made of them. She confided to me that sometimes her computer made her feel negative, angry and frustrated.

This didn't surprise me. I see it all the time. That's because I have been working with computers practically all my life, teaching people and developing products to show them how to use them effectively and enjoyably.

The truth is that those people who are connected to and have mastered how to use the Internet are better off than those who have not. The best rates on everything from insurance, savings and all manner of personal finance products are restricted to online deals. Many people now go online to use the many price comparison websites to check and compare prices. Companies cannot afford not to have a good Internet deal topping the best buy tables.

CHAPTER 1

20 Ways To Use Computers That Could Change Your Life

What Most People Are Using Computers For

The list is endless. Here is a summary of some of the ways people use their computers to change their lives. Some are small ways to improve everyday life whilst others are truly life-changing. I'll be going into more detail about some of them further on.

1 - Writing

They say there is a novel in every one of us and it's never been easier to write and publish one today. My father in law Harry is 90 years old and has used his computer to write his autobiography. Having mastered his computer, he's now got the bug and is writing his first novel as well!

But there's a host of other types of writing that people want to do. Whether it's letters to friends and family, formal letters, ideas, address books and much more.

2 - Calendar

Most computers will come with this function included. It means you can set up your diary and even get it to repeat events every day, week or year for you. Simply type in your dates and appointments and refer to it daily. You'll wonder how you managed before.

The down side is you will lose any pathetic excuse about forgetting your anniversary or an important birthday. Small price to pay!

3 - Managing Personal Finances

There are plenty of simple programs you can get to run on your computer that enable you to record your personal financial details. From bank accounts to standing orders, cheque payments, direct debits through to completing tax returns. People use other programs like "spreadsheets" to record and track their investment portfolios.

4 - Online banking

More people are ditching printed bank statements, cheque payments and calling into the bank to change arrangements. Now they do this over the Internet at the click of a mouse button. But beware! There are some security issues you need to know about that I will tell you about a little further on. Pop into your local bank and ask them about online banking and how you can take advantage of it.

5 - Digital Photos

I love this one! Your computer opens up a whole new world of fun and creativity with photography. With just a simple and cheap digital camera that stores photos on a card, which then plugs into your computer, you can store, print or share thousands of your photos. You can easily send them to friends or family over the Internet or use them in many other ways.

Plus you will also be able to manipulate the photos, get rid of red-eye, increase the light and yes, even crop out your ex-husband or wife from a photo! You will even be able to use a scanner to copy your old printed photos onto your computer so you can make the most of those as well.

6 - Ancestry

With so many libraries and archives being converted and stored on computer databases that are accessible on the Internet, it is no wonder that people are spending time tracing their family history records. It couldn't be simpler and websites like www.ancestry.co.uk are very popular.

7 - Video

OK, maybe you can't see yourself yet as the next blockbuster producer, but plenty of people are now filming home movies on digital video cameras that store video on a card that plugs into the computer.

I have a palm-sized video camera that fits into my pocket. I was invited to a friends wedding last summer and took the opportunity to take it with me. It was a lovely sunny day in a country house in the English countryside. All went well and the official wedding photographer did some great work but the person they hired to take a video never showed up. They were disappointed but it didn't spoil the day.

Since my video camera was so small, I kept it going without too much thought. Later, I was able to copy it to my computer and I spent a couple of hours editing out the worst bits and adding their favourite music and some titles. You can imagine their surprise and delight when I handed them their wedding DVD!

The creative opportunities are endless and, once you have made your own video, you can post it on the Internet at one of the free websites that keeps millions of videos for anyone to look at. There's more about this later but you can see an example of a quick video I put together that is on one of one of these websites at this link: www.youtube.com and then enter "KAZ Typing" in the search box.

Don't worry if you don't know how to do that yet. I will cover it further on.

As well as using video for fun, people are starting to experiment using their computers to produce videos on all sorts of topics for money. I do this myself and it's one of the things I teach my students. There's more about this further on.

So now you can take and edit your own wedding or any event videos to impress the family!

8 - Music

Stop thinking music CD's and start thinking digital downloads! This is one of the uses that will give you some serious fun and revolutionise the way you buy, store, organise and listen to your music.

9 - Audio Books

You can buy an audio book on a CD or tape to listen to without using your computer but with the advent of the digital music player and online music stores, buying an audio book couldn't be more convenient. Go onto the Internet and visit a music store website (a popular one is called iTunes). Not only can you buy music tracks to download with your credit card, you can choose from thousands of audio books to download and buy as well.

10 - Podcasts

Podcasts are catching on big time. They are like small radio programs. You can go to the same online music website and then select "podcasts". Many of these are free. You normally "subscribe" to a podcast. So, for example, if you subscribed to a weekly comedy podcast, you just click "Subscribe" once and then all future episodes will be downloaded automatically by your music software onto your computer via the Internet

The BBC records many of its radio programs onto podcast files that you can download. Then you can listen to them whenever you want on your computer or digital music player.

Anyone can make a podcast recording and post it to online music stores and you'll find thousands to choose from on every topic under the sun!

11 - Video Podcasts

All digital music players (like the iPod) play audio files, whether music or speech. Newer versions of these also have a small video screen built in as well.

This means people can choose to download video podcasts and they can watch and listen just like a TV show on their computer or digital music player.

Chapter 1 - 20 Ways To Use Computers That Could Change Your Life

12 - TV

As computers, TV and Hi-Fi come closer together, people are making the most of the new opportunities this presents.

I watch TV programs on my computer. I have installed some special software and plug in a normal TV aerial from a wall socket into a special connector that, in turn, connects to my computer. This means I can get live digital TV anytime I want on my computer.

More than that, I can access TV schedules over the Internet and set my computer to record TV programs to my hard disk. This allows me to watch them whenever I want.

I can also copy these TV programs onto my digital music player with its small video screen. These TV shows and films are stored along with all my songs, audio books and podcasts.

Now, when I find I have time to kill, on a train, plane or anywhere else, I can watch a film or TV program.

The hardware to get TV playing on your computer is available from various suppliers. Popular ones for the PC are www.TVstick.co.uk and for the Apple Mac www.miglia.com.

13 - Computer to TV

So now that computers can connect to one another, so can your computer and your TV. This is done with an extra "wireless" box plugged into the TV. The computer is WIFI enabled (see WIFI), which means it sends out wireless signals that are picked up by the TV box. I'll be showing you how this works further on.

So, with a little jiggery pokery, people can now look at the photos and videos on their computer and on their TV screen.

And that's not all. So far you know that you can download music, audio books and podcasts from your music store.

Now you can also download complete hi-definition movies! So having to go to the video rentals store is no more. Just go to the music store on the Internet, select and pay for a movie with your credit card and download the movie over your phone line directly onto your computer.

Then sit back and watch it on your computer or your TV.

14 - Games

Whether it's playing Solitaire or chess, or a "shoot 'em up" game, racing game or strategy game, there are literally thousands to choose from. People either buy a game on a CD ROM or they connect their computer to a games shop over the Internet. They simply pay by credit card. The game comes down the phone line and onto the computer and they're off! Some of the online games are massive multiplayer games. You connect to those games over the Internet along with thousands of people around the world and all play at the same time.

15 - Email

This is a bit like having an address book on your computer. It contains the address on the Internet of the email of your friends, family and contacts. In return you give them your special email address so they can set you up on their computer.

People simply call up an email address, then they type their message and press "send". The message is then automatically sent over the Internet and the next time your recipient turns on their computer to look for messages they will get yours. It's simple then for them to reply.

As well as typing messages you can add things you want people to get. For example, this could be one of your photos on your computer. It will simply get bundled up electronically, with your typed email message and be sent over the Internet, so your recipient can read your message and see the photo almost immediately.

16 - Telephone

Who'd have thought it? Now people are replacing the normal telephone with their computers! Why not? When you are connected to the Internet with your computer, it uses normal phone lines to send and receive information, so why not your telephone call as well?

The real attraction is that it's free to use!

Since you have paid for your Internet connection via the phone line, you can now call people up over the Internet who have a similar set up and speak to them for free.

So if you have a long lost aunt in Newcastle or Auckland, you can stay on the phone all day for free. Best of all, the same programs allow you to see each other as you are talking with the use of a small web camera. This camera is often built into the case of your computer, or you can buy one and plug it in. They are tiny and cheap to buy.

17 - Dating

The number of people using websites to find love and romance is soaring. More people are finding themselves alone, especially in later life where divorce is now endemic and partners have died.

Unless you are particularly single-minded and confident, the chances of meeting a new partner that you like are slim. This often depends on your colleagues at work (if you are still working), your social network (which may have halved with the loss of a partner) or potluck in bumping into someone you hit it off with.

Then there are the "lonely hearts" ads in the papers that nobody really trusts and are only prepared to use as a last desperate resort.

People now register with dating websites to extend their options. They get to interact with people in a safe way before deciding to meet up and the number of people to talk to is much higher than with any other way. I have friends who have new and happy relationships that originated from online dating that have literally changed their lives.

18 - Internet Surfing

Once your computer is connected to the Internet over your phone line, the world is your oyster! There are millions of websites around the world that people visit everyday. To make sense of them, they type what they are looking for into a special search box. This then searches sites from all over the world and responds with suggested sites to visit. All of this is almost instantaneous!

Plus people use their Internet connection to shop, do banking, book holidays and much, much more. Once you experience this yourself, you are limited only by your own imagination. Want to see satellite video of the earth? Want to watch a live camera on a cruise ship? Want to find the best price for your new camera? Want to see what people are saying about your local hospital? And on and on...

It's easy to lose yourself online and if you are not careful you'll end up wasting hours and becoming a recluse!

19 - Learning

Learning over the Internet (called e-learning) is opening up a world of new opportunities for people to learn new skills. People can learn everything from a new language to computer programming. The Open University (www.open.ac.uk) are pioneers in distance learning and many other traditional training providers have alternative e-learning options on the Internet. A large number of online learning options are available from Learndirect at www.learndirect.co.uk.

I do this with my KAZ Typing Tutor, where people simply purchase online access at my website www.kaz-type.com and then log on to the e-learning website www.kaz-type.com/kazonline with their email address and password.

20 - Making Money On The Internet

More and more people are looking for ways to make money using their computers and using the Internet. A whole industry has grown up around this and there are hundreds of websites promising to show people how to make an easy fortune "online" (using their computer and the Internet).

I love this topic as, if it is done well, there are simple and cheap ways for almost anyone to earn an extra income. They may be able to give up their jobs and earn a 6-figure salary and, yes, even earn millions from making their own products and marketing them online. If you are interested in learning about making money using computers, go to www.markmeakings.com where you will find lots of information to help get you started.

Conclusion

I've summarised some of ways people are using computers, with or without a connection to the Internet, and there is more detailed information further on. Yes, there is much to learn to become proficient, but you'll find once you begin to master the basics of one use, the rest will get a lot easier. Using your computer becomes intuitive and most of the time you will manage without too many problems. Then it becomes fun.

Be brave and get your feet wet!

CHAPTER 2

How To Choose The Right Computer And Get Off On The Right Foot

Choosing a Computer

Here's my top tip. Unless you are experienced, whatever computer you choose to buy, get it from someone who will be there afterwards to speak to and get help from if you find you need it.

Yes, I know you can get this or that computer cheaper on the Internet or one of the major stores. However, from the experience of many of my friends and students, unless you are confident and comfortable with computers, when you're pulling your hair out trying to get something to work, you'll be glad you spent that little extra money.

Always ask beforehand exactly what after sales support you can expect, during what hours it is available and check it is free. Or, if it does cost you, confirm how much. You can buy a cheap computer with "full support" only to find you have to call a premium phone number that costs a fortune to call. I suspect some suppliers make more on the phone call profits than from the sale of your computer. So take your time and take care.

Find someone who has a reasonable amount of experience and ask him or her to help you. You'll often see adverts on postcards in your local shop or in the local paper. Quite often these people picked up their experience and knowledge at work and now work part time from home. Ask your local computer shop and friends and contacts to recommend someone. The small amount of effort spent here is well worth it.

Windows PC or Apple Mac

The Personal Computer market began with the introduction of the IBM PC in 1981. Apple introduced their first personal computer called the "Macintosh" in 1984.

Over the years, two "standards" have emerged: PC's made by Apple using Mac Operating System 10 (OSX), and PC's made by everyone else including Dell, Gateway, Hewlett Packard, Advent and hundreds more running the Windows Operating System.

Both systems co-exist quite well together, both in hardware and in availability of software.

There's no clear winner here. It's a personal choice and I recommend taking a little time to consider this before you buy. It will affect your enjoyment of using computers for years to come. Once you are comfortable with one type of computer, it's hard to switch (but not impossible).

Here's some of the pros and cons of the 2 main types of computer:

Chapter 2 – Choosing Your Computer

Windows PC

The PC (**P**ersonal **C**omputer) is basically dumb until you load a software "program" onto it to tell it what to do. There is one program that comes with your PC and that sits in overall charge of the computer, regardless of what other programs are being used at any time, like a word processing program or maybe a photo manipulation program.

When you turn the PC on this program takes a little time to load in from the hard disk and makes your computer ready to undertake whatever task you want.

This program is called the "operating system" and on 95% of PC's this is made by Microsoft Inc and called "Windows". It doesn't matter which company makes the PC, whether it is Dell, IBM, COMPAQ or any one of a thousand other makes, what they all have in common is the Microsoft Windows operating system. This starts up when you switch them on.

Once Windows has automatically loaded, you can then start up your other programs (word processing, games, photos etc) and you can then see and work with them. However, Windows is running constantly in the background and looking after the central tasks like writing and reading data from your hard disk, monitoring your keyboard and much more.

Just to complicate things for us, Microsoft brings out new versions of its Windows PC operating system every so often. The first was many years ago and they have included Windows 3.1, Windows 95, Windows 98, Windows ME, Windows 2000, Windows 2003, Windows XP and Windows Vista. The chances are now you will be using either Windows XP or Vista.

Why Choose A Windows PC?

Since 95% of computers are Windows PCs, you know that your computer will be compatible with everyone else's. It will read files and run a greater number of programs than the alternative Apple Mac computer below.

I suppose you could call it the safe choice. Except in many ways it is the most dangerous. As the PC is so widely used, it is the main target for criminals and stupid people who have nothing better to do than try to get malicious programs onto your PC over the Internet in order to ruin it.

A whole industry had built up selling products that will protect you from harm – and if you use a PC you really will need them.

That said, if you take precautions, you would probably be very pleased with your new PC.

Apple Mac

Called the "Mac" (short for Mackintosh) by users, you either love or hate these computers. I will admit to making extensive use of PCs and Macs, and my personal choice is the Mac.

Like the PC, the Mac also needs an operating system program to run in order to be of any use. Instead of Windows, it is called OSX (Operating System 10). Just like Windows on the PC, it came in earlier versions from 8, 9 and now X (10). And within OSX there are new versions with fancy names like "Leopard" and "Tiger".

Confused? Don't worry, you don't need to know all about these, just the current version you have on your Mac.

It used to be that the Mac would only run a fraction of the programs you could run on a PC running Windows. Today, all that has changed. I find that the Mac can run all the programs I run on a PC. But if there are any that will not run, there are usually alternative programs to buy. If that doesn't work for you, they have conjured up a neat trick.

You can also run Windows on the new Mac computers!

Why Choose An Apple Mac?

Unlike PC's where you have lots of companies making different computers (hardware) and then adding Windows software to them, an Apple Mac and the operating system OSX are all made by a single company, Apple Computers.

That means the design is all in one place, seamless and more stable (in others words the Mac doesn't have the annoying habit of freezing up and having to be restarted every now and again).

Macs often cost more, but the quality, build and reliability can be worth it.

A major bonus is the security that's built in. I have not had to buy any extra products or tools to protect the Mac.

However, I don't know how long it will be before your friendly neighbourhood criminal starts to target Mac computers as well as Windows. I guess it is inevitable.

Conclusion

This really is a personal choice. People get quite passionate about it. A bit like supporters of 2 opposing football teams!

You won't be disappointed with either. Go and have a demonstration of both and see what "feels" right for you. Ask people you know what their experience is.

Alternative Operating Systems For PC's

There is an alternative to Windows that comes free. It's called "Linux" and it has been around in one form or another since 1991. It will run on any PC (not Apple Mac) and it's free. You can download it from the Internet (www.linux.com). It's still the outsider but it does most of the things Windows does, even if it does have a few rough edges.

Some manufacturers of PCs are fed up with Microsoft's virtual monopoly with Windows for the PC and they are starting to sell computers with Linux, instead of Windows, pre-installed. This reduces the price you pay as Linux is free. This is likely to be a growing trend in the future. Checkout www.dell.co.uk to see their Linux PC's.

What Computer "Hardware" To Buy

"Hardware" simply means the "hard" bits. The stuff you can touch. Like the main computer box, screen, keyboard and so on.

You also hear things you plug into your computer, like a printer, called "peripherals". More jargon, but you don't need to be aware of some of it.

When you are considering what hardware and peripherals to buy, it's the same principal for a PC or a MAC.

The Computer Box and Brain

This has all sorts of clever electronics inside, plus connection points to plug in everything from a printer and screen to cameras and games controllers.

Motherboard

Inside the computer is a main circuit board. This is called the Motherboard. All the other bits and pieces below connect to the Motherboard. Don't concern yourself about motherboards. It's just interesting to know this is how the computer is constructed.

Central Processing Unit (CPU)

At the heart of every computer is central processor unit (CPU). This chip is the "brain" and sits on the motherboard.

Chapter 2 – Choosing Your Computer

Sometimes, these are referred to a "single-core", "dual-core" or "quad-core". Dual core means the computer can do 2 jobs simultaneously. So while you are working on your photos, it can be checking your email and downloading stuff without slowing you down. Quad-core means it can do 4 jobs simultaneously.

The faster the chip works the more heat it kicks out and that's why you hear the fan working hard in the computer.

Technology is marching ahead all the time and what's super fast today will be considered a snail in 12 months time. So, ask what CPU you are getting and fork out for the best specification you can afford.

The main manufacturers Intel and AMD are equally good.

USB Connections

A USB (universal serial bus) connection is simply a standard way for devices to connect to your computer and most computers will have at least 2 of these connection points. As so many devices connect via a USB cable, I recommend you choose a computer with at least 4 USB connections to save you keep unplugging and plugging in devices.

Just to complicate things, they keep improving the speed of data transfer via USB connections. So older computers will have USB 1 connections. Some will have USB 2 and so on. Check what the current version is before you purchase and be sure to get it.

Firewire Connections

These connections are just like USB connections, except they use a different cable and plug at both ends. Firewire is many times faster at transferring data, so if you have large files to copy across, eg. a video from a video camera, you will be better off connecting it via Firewire than USB. Of course, both the computer and camera will have to have Firewire sockets (referred to as "ports").

Just like USB, make sure you have the latest version on your computer to get maximum benefits.

I recommend your computer have both USB and Firewire ports for maximum flexibility.

Bluetooth Connections

You've probably heard of this being used on mobile phones. It is simply a wireless connection. So, for example, if your mobile phone and your computer both have Bluetooth capabilities, they can "transmit" files to each other without the need for cables. This is how many people copy photos from their mobile phones onto their computers and how they copy music files from their computers onto their mobile phones.

Go to the help area of your computer and phone to find out how to turn Bluetooth on and off.

Memory - RAM

This means "random access memory". These are memory computer chips sitting on the motherboard that are used to temporarily store data and execute programs.

When you install a software program onto your computer, whether it be a game, accounts or photo program, it is stored on your hard disk. It remains on the hard disk even when the computer is turned off.

When you want to run the program, the computer loads the program from your hard disk into the computer memory (RAM) so that it can do its job. When you close the program, it frees up space in RAM for another one. The original program always sits on your hard disk ready to be used over and over again.

Ask what the current maximum RAM size is for the latest computers and, if you can afford it, get as close to this as possible. Having more RAM means your computer will work much faster, and you will notice this when you are playing with photos, large files, music and even on the Internet.

Cache Memory

This is just another form of memory. The computer uses this area to hold files on a temporary basis. It saves the computer having to keep reloading files and therefore the more you have, the faster your computer will be. Try to go for the current maximum or as near as possible.

CD/DVD Drive

You will want to play video DVDs and music CDs, copy things from them onto your computer and store new information on blank discs for backup.

Although they look the same, a CD ROM and a DVD are very different. The CD will normally be used for music or programs. A DVD stores many more times the data than a CD ROM. This is normally used to store movies or to copy files to and from your hard disk for backing up. I'll show you how to do this further on.

Your computer should have a built in CD Drive and a DVD Drive. Both drives should allow you to read files from them AND write files to them on blank discs.

It's common now for a single drive to handle both CDs and DVDs.

Hard Disk

This is built into your computer box. Currently most of these are mechanical devices that spin and record data on disk. Vast amounts of data can be stored, depending on the size you choose. Go for the largest you think you may need and then double it. I have always run out of disk space and you will too, especially if you are storing, music, photos and videos.

If you do run out of hard disk space, you could replace it with a larger one. This is not always straightforward. An easier way is to buy a second hard disk. This can be fitted inside the computer or, more commonly, simply plugged in via a cable to your computer box (external hard disk).

New types of "solid state" hard disks are now available and these can be better as they have no moving parts to fail. Currently these do not offer the same capacity as a "traditional" moving hard disk, but check when you buy as this will change and a solid state disk should be faster and withstand knocks much better.

The Computer Screen

There was a time when they were like huge TV's with massive backs on them. Now you should choose a flat screen as they are much easier to read and take up a lot less room.

I suggest you visit a large store and look and compare lots of screens to see what you like. For example, you can get a gloss or a matt finish.

Choose a wide screen format as you may want to play DVDs on it and you will see more information at one time as you use your computer.

Make sure you have the best screen resolution you can afford. This means more dots available so you get a clearer sharper picture. This is important for looking at pictures and photos.

Chapter 2 – Choosing Your Computer

When you pick a screen, check to ensure your computer can handle it. There is a "graphics card" full of computer chips plugged into the motherboard specifically to handle the screen display. If your screen has a very high resolution, the graphics card must be able to support it otherwise its capabilities may be lost. This is a bit like driving a fast sports car with a lawn mower engine under the bonnet!

You can spend a hundred to a thousand and what you buy should reflect what your use will be. Will you be spending hours looking at it? Will you want a larger screen so you can see more work at once?

Dual Screens

If you intend to have a lot of files or programs running at the same time, e.g. writing a letter, sending a mail, working with photos, then consider running 2 screens. The Apple Mac automatically allows you to plug in a second screen and you can double your "desktop" space on your computer. On a Windows PC, you may need to have a special graphics card installed to handle 2 screens. It doesn't cost much more and once you've tried this you'll wonder how you managed before.

When you buy a PC, you will need to ask for the internal graphics card to be replaced with a card that permits 2 screens. This should not add much to the cost.

Modem

This enables your computer to connect to the Internet over your telephone line. New computers usually have one of these built in. However, you may also receive one automatically when you sign up for an Internet Access Account with an Internet Service Provider (more later).

The Printer

Once you have typed your letter, or touched up your photos, chances are you will want to print them out.

There are 2 main types of printer. Inkjet and Laser.

Inkjet Printer

This connects via a cable to your computer box. It will normally come with a CD ROM that you insert into your computer and a program will automatically run. The computer will then say hello to your printer (install it on the hard disk) so it knows where to send your print jobs in the future.

Inkjet printers tend to be great value. However, they get their main profits from selling you ink cartridges that need replacing when empty. They give great results though. Have a demo in a store to see the best one for you.

Many of these printers also double as a fax machine, photocopier and a scanner. So as well as using them to print off a letter, you can send a fax, photocopy a document or even load in old photos or documents and scan them in to be stored on your computer. I use mine to scan old printed photos I had before the dawn of digital cameras, so my whole picture collection is on my computer.

Laser Printer

More expensive, laser printers operate like larger photocopiers. They give a more permanent result, unlike ink and can be black and white or colour. Printing costs tend to be higher, but the result is more professional.

My suggestion when you are starting out is to get a multipurpose inkjet printer and save looking at the laser printer until later. You may never need one.

Laptop vs Desktop Computers

Tricky. I use both. My desktop computer has a very large screen with a second screen set up. It also has the maximum memory and disk storage as I also work with video production.

I use my laptop when travelling and then upload the work to my desktop computer for "finishing" off, printing and filing.

You can buy very powerful laptop computers, which means that you don't necessarily need a desktop computer. If you are tempted, compare the specifications of the laptop computer with a desktop computer to get as close as possible. As a minimum, compare the speed of the processor, the amount of memory they hold and the size of the hard disk. You will also normally be able to plug a large screen into a laptop, if you want to use it as your desktop machine with a bigger display.

It's all about how you want to use a computer and your personal preference. Try to pick a manufacturer with good tech support. Consider HP, Toshiba, Dell or Apple.

Here's another top tip. Keep all the laptop packaging and disks safe. Should you change your mind and want a desktop computer later, you can repackage it and sell it on an Internet auction site like EBay and use the money towards another computer!

Consider these issues before you run out and buy:

Laptop Pros:

Portability
They take up much less room
Are powered by mains electricity or batteries
They are great when you are away from your office
They look good
Great for students
Tend to come with built in microphone and speakers
Sometimes come with built in web camera in the screen surround

Laptop Cons:

Generally less powerful than a desktop computer
Limited battery life (although you can carry a spare)
Can get hot
More expensive than desktops
Limited scope to expand them
Not made to be taken apart

Desktop Pros:

Powerful
Easy to expand
Great for games, photos and videos
Cheaper than laptops
Easy to take apart

Desktop Cons:

They are big
Not portable
Heavy
Can be more complex to set up
Often no built in speakers, camera or microphone

WIFI (wireless network)

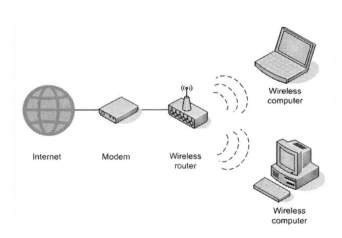

In the case of home use, you may have more than 1 computer and they may need to share a printer and a single connection to the Internet. You might also want to copy files or documents from one computer to another. For example, you may bring a laptop home and want to connect it to your desktop PC and copy across some work you were doing. You can connect all of these devices together in a "network". It wasn't so long ago that people talked about linking computers together in a network and panic would set in.

The good news is that recent versions of Microsoft Windows make this much easier. The Mac has always been a breeze to network.

Chapter 2 – Choosing Your Computer

Previously, you would have to buy lots of cables and start knitting it all together and it was very messy.

But all that's changed with the invention of wireless or WI-FI technology. This simply means a wireless connection without cables.

You buy a small peripheral called a "router" or "home hub". This sits independently of your computers and is always switched on and connected to the Internet.

Each of your computers is "WI-FI" enabled. In other words they have a wireless adapter or card built in. When you switch on your computer, the home hub receives a wireless signal from it. It can then "connect" your computer to the Internet without the need for cables.

If you have a WI-FI enabled laptop, you can take it anywhere within wireless range of the home hub and connect to the Internet. Maybe you want to use it in the kitchen or garden.

So far so good. Now you have a second WI-FI enabled computer at home. You turn this one on and the home hub detects that one as well. As a result, both computers can connect wirelessly to the Internet at the same time via the home hub.

Since the home hub connects each computer to the Internet, it can also connect each computer to the other. So, for example, you could do some typing on a laptop computer away from home. Later at home, when you turn your laptop on, the home hub will pick up the signal. Assuming you have another computer connected wirelessly to the home hub, you can copy your work from your laptop to the other computer.

You may need to set up files on each computer to allow them to be shared across the network. This is called setting the "sharing permissions". The simplest way is to decide which files you want to share. To make them available, right click on the folder or the file, select "sharing" and "Sharing and Security" for Windows XP or "Share" for Windows Vista and follow the instructions.

As well as having computers connected wirelessly to the home hub, you can also have printers connected in the same way. For example, you may have one printer that you want to share between all the computers on your network. In this case your printer also needs to be Wi-Fi enabled.

A home hub will allow you to mix Windows PC's with Apple Mac's at the same time.

To summarise, in addition to your computers you will need the home hub and a broadband phone line. Most broadband providers provide home hubs for free or as an upgrade. You can also buy them at your local computer store or online.

A popular make is Belkin (www.belkin.co.uk, select "networking" and then "wireless"). Select one with at least four Ethernet ports. Ethernet ports are where you plug a cable in. So for example, if you have a printer that is not Wi-Fi enabled, you can still use it but instead of connecting it wirelessly to the home hub, you connect it with a cable and it can then be shared between computers.

Sometime the wireless range can be an issue so look for one that can take an external aerial.

Setting this up is fairly straightforward but you will have to study the instructions that come with it. Usually you just pop the CD into the computer and then follow the instructions on-screen. It wouldn't hurt to have someone on the end of the phone to call if you need assistance beforehand.

Games consoles like the Xbox and WII that you play on your TV also connect wirelessly to the home hub in order to get onto the Internet to download new games.

You can buy a TV device that connects to the home hub that also allows you to show your photos or videos on the TV. You could even download a movie from the Internet and watch it on TV.

This is something for you to look into and have fun with once you have mastered your computer. It's not hard, so be patient.

Wireless Hotspots

If you have a laptop computer that is wireless enabled (it has a wireless network card installed inside) you can not only use it to connect to your wireless network at home or work, you can also connect it to any one of thousands of Wireless Hotspots around the country.

Most major telephone companies have set up wireless hubs in airports, public buildings and the like. When you turn your laptop on, it will try to find a local wireless network to connect to. So, for example, if you are waiting on a mainline station, it may pick up a BT wireless hub in range in the station. You will usually have to pay to connect to the service and you can often do this with your credit card before using your computer. Sometimes you can purchase access in advance.

To get a list of all BT Hotspots and to purchase vouchers for use when you are travelling, go to http://btopenzone.hotspot-directory.com

It's quite common for hotels to provide their own Wireless Hotspot, often for free. You simply turn on your laptop, select wireless settings and click on the link to get connected to the Internet.

WIMAX

In some ways WIMAX is similar to WI-FI in that a base station (the home hub or router) radiates a signal to a user's computer to give them access to hi-speed Internet access and to share files between computers.

However, WI-FI only reaches about 100 metres, whereas a WIMAX base station can reach 2-3 kilometres. This opens up possibilities for you to use your computer in this way much further afield.

A WIMAX base station is more likely to be provided by an Internet Service Provider or telephone company. So for example, you and others could use your computers in this way anywhere in your local town.

My favourite island in the sun, Mauritius, is already there. People just plug in a wireless Wimax modem into their laptop and get high speed Internet access anywhere on the island.

Upgrading Or Replacing Your Computer?

Often people will decide to trash an old computer and upgrade to a new one. Sometimes this is a clear-cut decision because a new computer will have more features and greater speed than the old. This may be important if you are widening the range of use for the computer, to run a business or to do video editing for example.

However, if all you are experiencing is a slow and sluggish computer and a lack of hard disk space, it's worth considering making changes to your current computer to see if it will get you the same result for less cost.

The price tag isn't the only cost. There is also the time and effort to migrate your information to a new computer, which is not trivial.

The other bonus of keeping with your current computer is that all of your current programs and data are working fine and if you transfer to a new computer you may have some hoops to jump through (rarely is anything as simple as you expect).

Improving Your Current Computer

Defragment Your Hard Disk

Over time the computer will slow down. This is because files and data are written, deleted and written again all over the hard disk.

Frequently, a single file is stored in pieces all over the place. You don't see this happening, but it takes longer for the computer to fetch the parts and piece them all together for you. You experience this as a "slow" computer.

A quick way to improve performance is to "defrag" (de-fragment) your hard disk. This means taking all the files and re-writing them in order with no spaces, nicely and neatly. On a Windows PC go to "Start" and "Help" and type in "defrag" to the search box for instructions. You leave this running on your computer and come back after an hour or so.

The Apple Mac is more intelligent in storing data and you don't need to defrag the hard drive.

Increase Your Hard Disk Capacity

Or course, it may be that you are running out of hard disk. In which case you could have it replaced with a larger one, or simply buy an additional hard disk. This can be fitted in the computer box or plugged in via a USB or Firewire plug with it sitting on your desk. Hard disks are cheap to buy nowadays.

Increase Internal Memory (RAM)

Generally, the more internal memory you have the faster your computer will be. There are 2 types to look at. RAM (Random Access Memory) and Cache memory. Don't get hung up on what they do, just find out how much you have, how much the computer can hold and then get the maximum. This can really speed things up.

To get a rundown of what your computer consists of:

On a Windows Vista PC, select the Windows icon in the bottom left corner of the desktop, Computer and them System Properties.

On a Windows XP PC, select Control Panel and then System.

On an Apple Mac, click on the Apple logo, then "about this Mac" and then "more info".

You may need someone to look inside to see what chip sockets are available to find out how much the computer can accommodate.

Chapter 2 – Choosing Your Computer

Fix-it Utilities

Another reason for sluggishness is that over time, you will install more and more programs and many of these will make more demands of your computer's processor in an inefficient way.

Think of it like spinning plates. A new computer has the operating system program (Windows or Mac OSX) and a few programs running so it only has to keep a few plates spinning at once. Gradually the number of plates increases with the number of programs added and this increasingly affects processor resources.

So before you give up on your current PC it's worth considering buying a specialist software program that will examine your Windows PC and make changes for you to make all of these functions run more smoothly and speed them up. A popular one for the PC is "Fix-it Utilities" (www.avanquest.com/uk)

Upgrading To A New Computer

Remember those operating systems? Windows and Mac OSX. Well they develop these over time so that a new version is released every year or so with more bells and whistles.

Windows started with Windows 95, Windows 98, Windows ME, Windows 2000, Windows XP and Windows Vista.

Mac started with OS8, OS9 and now OSX and even then there are different versions of OSX called "Tiger" and "Leopard". By the time you read this book there may well be new ones.

If you are buying a new computer none of this matters as you will always buy the latest Windows or Mac OSX. However, when you move from an old computer, it may be that some of your programs will not work on the new operating system. In other words old programs may be incompatible with the new version of the operating system.

The manufacturers work hard to avoid this problem and always try to make new operating system programs "backwards compatible". In other words, they make them able to run all of your old programs.

However, in a small number of cases your old programs may no longer work. You can usually go back to the company that makes the program you want to use. They may have a new version that does run on the new operating system. You may have to pay a small charge to get the new program.

Copying Data From Old To New Computers

You can simply connect the 2 computers via a cable and use the copy function in Windows or Mac to transfer the contents of your old computer to your new one. Alternatively, you can use a special program to make the process simpler and easier. One such program is PC Mover www.laplink.com and a search online or a visit to your local computer store will reveal others.

Bear in mind you cannot easily upgrade from a PC to a MAC or vice versa.

Be sure to deal properly with the computer you are discarding. Whether you intend to pass it on or have it recycled, it will still contain all of your files and information.

Once you are confident that all your data has successfully been transferred to your new computer, as an added safety precaution, take backup copies of the important data from your old machine. See the section on backup for this.

Next you need to "wipe" the hard drive on your old computer so all of your data is completely removed. You don't want a stranger who acquires the computer to have access to your files.

There are many cheap programs you can buy to do this for you and it is worth the time and effort. Go onto the Internet and search for "disk clean". There you will find a wide choice of programs to use.

Simply deleting files will not work. Although their entry is deleted on the hard disk, the actual file remains behind until it is overwritten when new data needs the space.

Remember, that even if you smash your old computer, it will still be possible to recover data from it.

Going Green

Millions of computers are left switched on, idling away for hours and this wastes a huge amount of energy; energy that will ultimately cost you money.

Configuring your computer for energy efficiency takes a few minutes, but it will save you money, wear and tear and prolong the life of some of your computer's components. This becomes even more essential if you use a laptop computer as it will increase the battery life.

On a Windows PC most of the power saving options can be accessed by clicking on "Start" and then "Control Panel".

Chapter 2 – Choosing Your Computer

Usually there are 4 "states" your PC computer can be in:

Ready: this is when the computer is in normal use.

Standby: where after a pre-set period of inactivity the computer is not being used, the screen and disk drives are switched off. They come back on automatically when a key is pressed or the mouse is moved.

Suspend: the lowest power consumption mode, where the machine is not being used and the central processor remains active but everything else shuts down until a key is pressed or mouse moved. This is commonly used in laptops when the computer is left switched on and the lid is closed. Opening the lid brings the computer back to life and you carry on where you left off.

Hibernate: let's say you were working with 3 programs and in the middle of some important work and you didn't want to have to save and close down everything and spend time starting the programs and opening the files next time you switched your computer on. Switching off the computer in hibernation mode will cause all the details of what you were working on to be recorded.

Then next time you switch your computer on, you see the same screen as before with everything as it was and just continue where you left off.

On A Mac Computer: you'll find these power saving options by clicking on the Apple icon and selecting "preferences" from the drop down menu. You will see two easy presets when you then select "Energy Saving". So for example you can set your screen to turn off after 2 minutes of inactivity and the hard disk after 5 minutes.

Recycling

New European regulations are now in force to compel computer manufacturers to take back old equipment and recycle it. Check this at the time of purchase.

Don't throw your old computer away or take it to land fill. There are people that will professionally "wipe" your data from the hard disk, refurbish it and provide it to people in other parts of the world who need them. Checkout www.computeraid.org.

CHAPTER 3

How To Choose And The Best Way To Buy Your Software Programs

So What Is A "Software Program"?

"Software" simply means the stuff you can't actually touch. Mostly this means computer "programs".

There are tens of thousands of different "software programs" written by individuals, companies and organisations. You may find a program written by a school child at home that helps you make funny pictures on your computer. Then there will be programs written by multi-billion corporations like Microsoft that enable you to keep a diary.

Pop down to your local computer store to see the racks of software boxes containing all sorts of programs for you to use. In the pack you will find a CD ROM. You take that home, pop it into your computer and the "program" that is on it will automatically take you through the steps you need to get it onto your hard disk so you can start to use it. This process is called "installing" the software.

Without a program running on your computer, it is essentially "dumb". Turn it on and nothing would happen.

Once the program is "installed" onto the hard disk in your computer box, it is "run" or started up. The program is then loaded from the hard disk into the computer's memory (RAM or random access memory). The separate brain (CPU processor chip) then performs the instructions of the program that are now sitting in the computers memory.

When you switch off your computer or when you close a program down, everything that is on your hard disk remains safe. However, the contents of the computer's memory are emptied. So, the next time you switch on or you want to use the program again, it is "run" and reloaded onto the computer's memory once more.

Don't get hung up on this. It all happens automatically for you at the click of a mouse. It just might help you to understand what's going on in the background.

Bright sparks that are known as "software developers" or "programmers'" spend vast amounts of time and money creating a series of simple instructions for the computer to perform. Programs consist of thousands, and sometimes millions, of instructions. So, for example, when you click your mouse to print a document, the computer may have "executed" a thousand lines of instructions ("code") to make it happen. Since it can perform these in millionths of a second, it is transparent to you and looks simple.

A program could be designed and written in code for the computer to understand that manages your accounts, touches up photos, plays a game, writes a letter and so on.

Programmers lump all this code together into the "program" your computer loads in a language that it understands. Since this can be very complex, it is common for "bugs'"or errors to be in a program that have gone undetected despite exhaustive testing before the program is put on the market. This is why you will often get free program updates over the Internet for Windows and Apple OSX delivered to your computer automatically. Quite often when you switch your computer off Windows will interrupt you to say an update has been automatically downloaded over the Internet to your computer when you were connected to the Internet. It will then install it before it switches off your machine.

Always accept these updates, as they not only fix bugs in the program that can cause your computer to hang up or crash, they may also contain new security features to combat computer viruses and the like.

Interestingly, software "bugs" aren't so crucial on a home PC, but you have to imagine how much more testing and how much more critical they could be if they were found in the software programs that are running on computers that control a 747 or the Space Shuttle!

You will find programs either pre-loaded onto your hard disk when you buy your computer, on CD ROMs that you can buy, or on the Internet that you can download to be stored directly onto your hard disk. You can even go onto the Internet to "run" a program on a distant computer that you see on your computer screen without the need to get any software onto your hard disk.

How To Buy Your Software Programs

Let me illustrate this for you by showing you how customers can purchase one of my own software programs. This is typical of what you can expect.

KAZ "Learn To Type In Just 90 Minutes" typing tutor ("KAZ" is short for Keyboard A-Z) is used by over a million people around the world, including schools, colleges, and universities and in business and government.

Having finally cracked how to make learning to type a cinch for anyone from 5 to 95, I then designed the software and we then "wrote the program" so that people could use it on their computer, whether for PC or Mac, simply by following the instructions on the screen (the program).

Let's say you were tired of typing with 2 fingers, looking up and down and correcting mistakes, and you wanted to be able to type like a professional but without taking the normal hours of boring typing drills, and instead you learn to type in just 90 minutes.

You've heard about KAZ and now all you have to do is decide how you want to get the software and use it.

The options available are:

Buy The CD Rom From Your Local Computer Shop

You could visit a computer store or shop, find the KAZ box containing the CD ROM, take it home, pop the CD into your computer and follow the on-screen instructions to install it on your hard disk and off you go.

OR

Buy The CD Rom From A Website Shop

You could go to any number of software stores on the Internet that sell KAZ (including our own at http://www.kaz-type.com), fill in an order form with your credit card details and delivery address on-screen. Your credit card payment is automatically and securely cleared in seconds and the money sent to us together with your order and we normally post the CD to you the same day.

OR

Download It Over The Internet

You could visit our website (http://www.kaz-type.com), and instead of purchasing a CD ROM, you can "download" the software program then and there over your telephone line and have it automatically installed onto your hard disk to use immediately. All this does is take the same program you would get on a CD and, instead of posting it to you, we simply "send" the electronic contents of the program over the Internet and down your telephone line directly onto your computer.

Downloading software this way is more convenient and it means you get your software immediately, without having to go out in the rain! You don't get the pretty box and CD to keep, but then once you have it on your computer you don't need them anyway.

This way of buying software is rapidly becoming the norm and as a result larger stores like PC World are stocking less software CD's as demand for them diminishes.

Be aware that not all software programs are available this way and you may have to make a trip to the computer shop to get them.

Chapter 3 – Choosing Your Software

OR

Use It Immediately Online

If you didn't want to buy the program to install on your own computer, you can buy access to use it (called a "subscription") over the Internet. This would be running on our computer (sometimes called a "server" as it "serves" up software).

This is called "e-learning" or "online learning". It takes away all the hassle associated with having to install software from a CD or via a download onto your hard disk. It is very popular with schools and companies and we have hundreds of schools training thousands of pupils using KAZ online over the Internet.

So when you are at my online store, you will see this choice listed along with buying the CD or buying a download of the software.

This method of "renting" access to software gives you the freedom to access KAZ from any computer anywhere in the world. You simply go to the special KAZ Internet website (http://www.touchtypeonline.com), enter your email address and special password and, hey presto, the program runs immediately across the Internet on your computer, in just the same way as if it was running from your own hard disk.

In this case, instead of installing the software onto your hard disk, it is stored on our hard disk on a computer that you access over the Internet. It's just like using it from your computer, but instead you are using it from ours over the Internet.

What's Best For You

So the KAZ example shows you how people are choosing to buy and use software and the flexible ways that software developers have come up with to make it easy for them.

When you are choosing a program (software) to buy, check that it's designed for a PC or Mac depending on what computer you have. You will also find a "spec" or "specification" of computer that you need so that you can run the software. This is normally a minimum amount of computer memory, enough space on your hard disk to "install" it, a CD ROM drive, the version of Windows or Mac OSX it will run on and anything else necessary.

Most software you find will be designed to run on most specifications of machine, but it's worth checking to save a return visit for a refund later.

What Software Do You Want?

Here's a summary of software. I will give you more details of some of these further on.

Before you do anything, first find out what software is already "installed" on your computer. Most manufacturers know what people want and, to make their computer more attractive to buy, will give you software for free to use straight away.

To see what programs are already installed and ready to use:

On a Windows PC click on START (or the Windows icon at the bottom left of the screen) and then PROGRAMS

On an Apple Mac, move your mouse down to the bottom of the screen and you will see the "dock". You will find little pictures (icons) representing each program. Just run your mouse over them and you will see the title of each one.

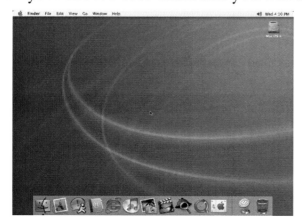

Not all programs are in the dock though and to see the rest, click on "Go" in the tool bar at the top of the screen and then select "Applications". This will reveal a list of programs already installed in a drop down menu.

Office Suite

The vast majority of people will use an "office suite" of programs for their basic needs. This package of programs usually contains a minimum of a word processor, spreadsheet and presentation package, but will often have more.

Microsoft "Office" is the best selling office suite and since most people use it, exchanging documents with other people is a breeze. I use this package and the documents I create with it on my PC will also work on my Apple Mac and vice versa. However, MS Office isn't the only choice. "Open Office" (www.openoffice.org) does much the same as MS Office but it is free. Checkout Star Office as well at http://www.sun.com/software/star/staroffice/index.jsp

These little known secrets are worth exploring as they look and feel like MS Office, work on Windows and Mac computers and the files they create are compatible. To find more alternatives go to www.download.com and search for individual programs like "word processor".

Word Processor

These programs will enable you to type, edit, store and print letters and documents. The most widely used is called Microsoft "Word". You can buy this separately but it usually comes as part of Microsoft Office.

Spreadsheet

This is a grid program where you can enter numbers and perform automatic calculations on them. For example, you could set it up to list a valuation of shares, calculate a price list, record your accounts and plenty more. The most widely used is called Microsoft "Excel" and normally comes as part of Microsoft Office.

Graphics

Microsoft "Publisher" enables you to produce anything from letterheads, posters, and calendars to anything pictorial.

Digital Photos

Your computer should come with software to enable you to store and print photos. However, if you have a digital camera that connects to your computer, the chances are it will also come with its own "software" on a CD ROM that you can install. These programs allow you to manipulate photos, enhance them, make calendars with them and a whole lot more.

There are literally too many programs to mention. Talk to friends and contacts about the software they use to see if any would be useful for you to get (and since they have them, they can shortcut some learning time for you with their own experience!).

Conclusion

If you are starting from scratch, get yourself an Office Suite of programs. These will handle most of your basic day-to-day tasks.

Once you have mastered the general operation of them, like starting and closing programs, typing, printing and saving documents, you will find this experience helps you as you start to use new programs for other things. Most programs are designed to work in a similar way, so learning to use new programs becomes intuitive.

Basic Software For The Internet

There are 2 main programs you need and both will almost always be provided free with your computer. A "Web Browser" and "Email Client".

Web Browser

There are millions of websites on the Internet. When you are looking at them it is referred to as "surfing" or "browsing" hence a "web browser" program. Most browser programs look similar and do more or less the same job. For Windows PC's another Microsoft software product that is widely used is called "Internet Explorer". For the Mac a popular one is "Safari".

On the Windows PC, hackers and virus writers target Microsoft Internet Explorer, and although new security measures are in place, you might prefer to use an alternative browser as I do. Try "Firefox". It's free and you can download it at http://www.mozilla.com/firefox.

Email Client

You use this program to type up and send and receive electronic messages to other people. On a PC, again Microsoft use their program called "Outlook" or "Outlook Express" and on the Mac it's a simpler program title called "Mail".

There is more about these programs further on.

Digital Music

The most popular software is called iTunes. It is made by Apple for the Apple Mac computer and also for Windows PC. Usually, you will connect to the Internet and go to the iTunes website to download and install this free program onto your computer. You can then pop all your music CD's into your computer and the program will load them onto your hard disk. You can also visit the iTunes shop on the Internet to choose music to buy and download into your collection. There is more information further on.

Freeware And Shareware Programs

Believe it or not, some people write programs and give them away for free. When you are browsing the Internet you will find websites that list these programs and allow you to download them to your computer. This is called "Freeware".

Then there is "Shareware". This is where you can download and use a program for free, but if you like it you are requested to make a donation. This is usually optional. Sometimes, you are allowed to use the program for free for a limited time. Then you can decide to purchase it if you like it.

Popular websites to get you going include: http://www.download.com, http://www.tucows.com, www.jumbo.com

As with all things on the Internet, you need to be aware of security issues when downloading programs. Please read the separate section on security.

CHAPTER 4
Getting Started Using Your Computer

The Desktop

No matter whether you have a Windows PC or an Apple Mac, the principles are the same. The way you do things varies though.

When you turn your computer on, you have to wait while it loads the operating system program into its memory so it can start working.

You then see what is called the "Desktop". Think of this like your physical desktop.

Windows desktop

Apple Mac Desktop

Usually, you will accumulate items on the desktop. They will be files, folders and shortcuts to running programs (more shortly). They are represented by tiny pictures that are called "icons".

Chapter 4 – Getting Started

Desktop Wallpaper

But first, there will be a "background" colour or picture taking up the screen (desktop). This is known as the "wallpaper". You can change this to another colour or perhaps a photo stored on your computer to personalise your desktop.

On a **Windows XP PC**, simply place your cursor anywhere on the desktop and click the right button on your mouse. Then select Properties and Wallpaper from the drop down menu and follow the instructions.

On a **Windows Vista PC**, right click anywhere on the desktop and select "Personalize", then choose Desktop.

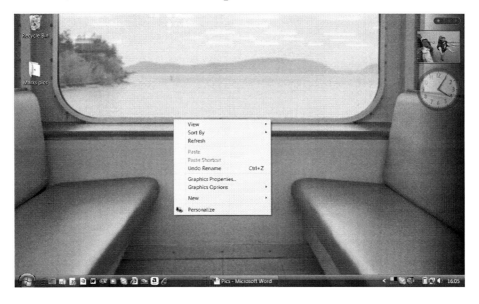

On a Mac, click on the little picture of an apple in the top left of the screen and select system preferences from the drop down list. Once this opens up, you can see all of the system preferences you can set. For now click on "desktop and screensaver" and follow the instructions.

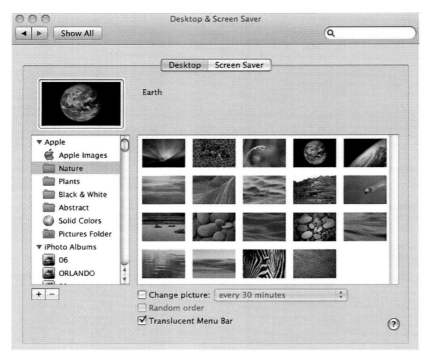

Alternatively, place your cursor anywhere on your Mac desktop, hold the "CTRL" down and click the mouse. Then select "Change Desktop Background"

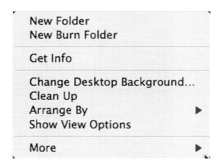

Screensaver

When you are changing your "wallpaper" you will also come across settings for a "screensaver". This is a picture (or series of pictures) that display automatically if you leave your computer on and stop using it for a length of time. This is to protect the screen (and it looks good). The screensaver disappears when you start to use the computer again.

I have all my personal photos stored on my computer and choose to have these rotate as my screensaver.

Running Software Programs

Once you've talked to your family and friends and shopped around, you'll probably have list of different programs you want to use on your computer. Maybe you will buy a game, a program to design and print greetings cards, a program to design posters and letterheads etc.

After you have installed these onto your computer by inserting the program CD ROM or having downloaded them from the Internet and followed the instructions on the screen, they will be sitting in your "programs" folder on a PC or the "applications" folder on a Mac.

There are 2 main ways to find and start each program. The first is to find the folder on your hard disk that contains the program and double click on it.

On a PC click on START at the bottom left of your screen, select "programs" and you will see a list of all your programs. Locate the one you want and double click your mouse on it.

On a Mac, from the desktop select "go to" from the top toolbar, then choose "applications" (programs). Then click on the one you want from the list.

When you install most programs, you will be asked if you want to have an "icon" placed on your desktop. This is a tiny picture or graphic that represents the program. This is also called a "shortcut" as when you click on it, it goes straight to the program and runs it.

Turning The Computer Off

At the end of a session, you normally turn your computer, screen and connected "peripherals" like printers off.

On your Windows PC click on the START button at the bottom left and select "close down". You will see several options. As well as a straight power off, you can "hibernate". This is quite useful. Let's say you are in the middle of typing a letter using Microsoft Word. When you select hibernate when you switch the computer back on, it will automatically load everything you need to carry on typing where you left off.

On the Mac, click on the apple icon at the top of the screen and select "shut down". If you use you Mac a lot, you could select "sleep" instead. This shuts down most of the power and puts the computer into standby mode. Just click the mouse and it all springs to life again.

There is more about using these options to save power and be green further on.

CHAPTER 5

How To Organise Your Computer, Work With And Protect Your Files

Once you spend a little time learning how to use the basic functions of the Windows or Mac Operating System program (the "OS" for short), you will see that they organise your data and programs on the hard disk into "folders". These are a bit like the folders in a filing cabinet.

Creating Folders

Windows or Mac OSX will have already named and created lots of folders it needs and some for you to use to start with.

The most important for you are:

The folder names are "My Documents" for Windows XP, or "Documents" in Windows Vista.

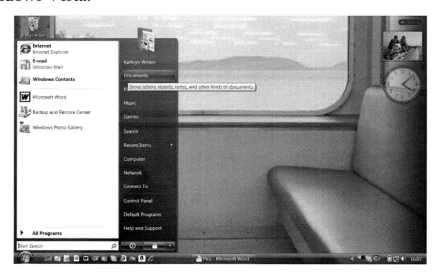

And Mac – the folder named "Documents"

Chapter 5 – Organise Your Computer

Now the great thing is that you can create more folders to store within this "documents" folder. You will be able to create a new folder and give it a name. So, for example, you could create a host of new folder names under the main Documents folder, e.g. "Letters", "photos", "pension", "work", "private" and so on. This makes it easy for you to find your documents later on.

How To Create A New Folder On The PC

Every time you create a new file, whether it's a letter or a spreadsheet file with your stamp collection in it, you will be able to choose **where** the computer stores it on your hard disk.

To create a folder for your Windows PC, click on the START button. Select "My Computer" and a new window will open showing you what folders you have. Your hard disk is normally referred to as "drive c", so click on this to get a picture of all the folders.

Then move down to the folder called "My Documents" and click on it to reveal all the various folders within it.

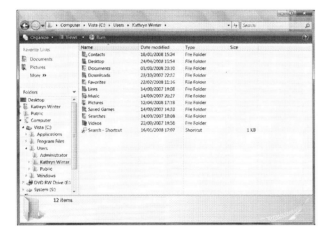

This makes it easy to find documents. You will always start by looking in the main folder, "Documents", where you will then see a list of folders that you have created. You then open up the relevant folder to see a list of corresponding files. When you have selected the Documents folder, right click your mouse and choose 'Make New Folder', type in a name and press Enter.

If you make a mistake, right click your mouse on the folder you created and select 'Delete Folder'. If there are files in the folder, you will be asked to confirm you want them deleted at the same time.

If you delete any files by mistake, you will find them in the 'Recycle' folder on the desktop. To recover a deleted file, simply double click on the Recycle folder to open it. Click on the deleted file and hold the mouse button down. Then drag your mouse with the file to the desktop and release it.

How to Create A New Folder On The Apple Mac

On the Apple Mac, click on "Go" from the toolbar at the top of the desktop. Select "home" to go to the main folder where your personal files are stored. You can click on any folder to see the contents. To create a new folder, click on "File" in the top menu bar and then "New Folder" and type in a name for it.

Don't worry if you create folders in the wrong place. You can click on them and select delete or press the delete key and have another go.

Once you have created some new folders, you can tell programs like Microsoft Word that you want the letter you have typed to be stored in a particular folder so you can find it easily later on.

Creating Shortcuts

If you have a program or a document or file stored on your hard disk and you frequently want to use or refer to it, you normally have to navigate around your hard disk to find it. You start by looking at the main record for the hard disk, which shows all the various folders of programs and data listed. Then you work your way down through levels of folders to locate it.

Let's say I have created a document I need to refer to every day. It's called "my notes" and I created it with Microsoft Word. It's stored in the folder on my hard disk called "private files" and in turn the folder, private files, is stored along with other folders under the main folder called "my documents".

One way to access this file, is to start the Word program, select "Open File" and use it to click around folders to find and open this document.

However, there is another way. Simply locate the document on the hard disk folder and double click on it.

Chapter 5 – Organise Your Computer

In the same way, you can start a program by locating it in the program folder and double clicking your mouse on it.

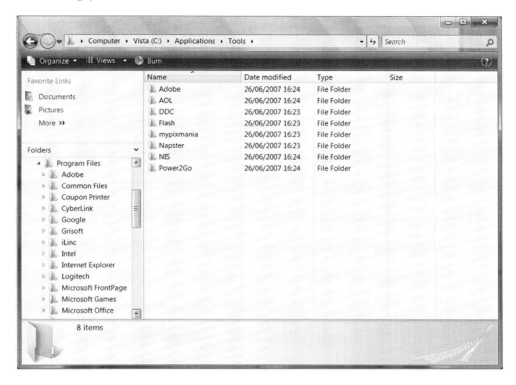

Then you select the folder you want and click on it to reveal the list of files inside

.

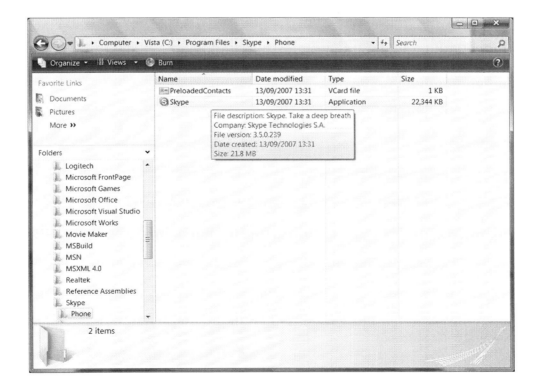

Then you locate the file you want from the list. If it's a program, you double click on it with your mouse to run it. If it's a document, double clicking on it should open up the program it was created with, so you can see or work on it.

It's much easier to create a "shortcut" to this file and place it on the computer desktop. By clicking on the shortcut, the computer goes straight to the file and actions it for you.

Creating a shortcut to the file is simple. Once you locate the file on the hard disk, press your right mouse key over it and from the small drop down menu select "make shortcut". This will place a shortcut in the same folder. Then simply click on it and drag it onto the desktop and release the mouse button. All you need to do in future is click on it to immediately open the file (or run the program if you have one selected).

The Apple Mac computer works with the "dock" which is a line of icons at the bottom of the screen containing shortcuts. To create a shortcut, click on the "finder" program icon on the dock to open a window of folders and files on the hard disk.

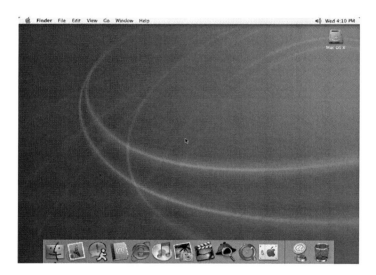

Locate the file you want, click and hold the mouse button down and simply drag this to the dock and release the mouse. Hey presto, shortcut created! To remove a shortcut from the dock, click and hold the mouse on it and drag it to the desktop and it will disappear with a "puff".

Another way to have a shortcut on the Apple Mac desktop instead of in the dock is to locate the file, then hold the "ctrl" key down and click on it to reveal choices. Select "make alias". This creates a shortcut that you drag onto the desktop.

Chapter 5 – Organise Your Computer

Deleting Files

You can delete files, folders and shortcuts easily. This is done on a Windows PC by making use of the Recycle Bin. Simply drag your unwanted files to the recycle folder.

Double click the Recycle folder to reveal the contents.

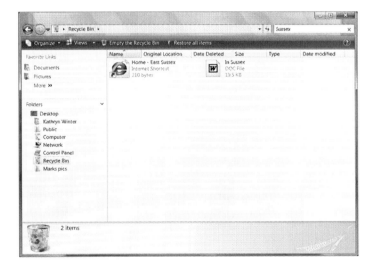

On the Mac, use the Trashcan at the bottom right end of the dock.

Click on it to reveal the contents.

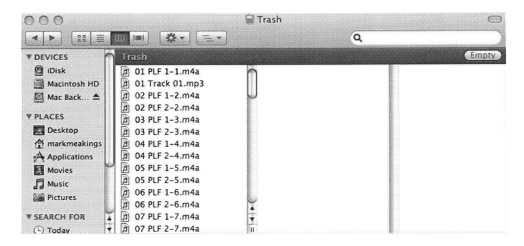

The principle is identical. When you delete a file, it is moved to this place. It is "marked" for deletion but not actually removed yet from your computer. That's to give you a second chance to change your mind. By opening up these folders, you can see the files you have "deleted" over time and you can "recover'" any of them by simply clicking on them and dragging them out of the folder and back onto your desktop or other folder.

When you are certain you want to "properly" delete the files, simply right click your mouse on the recycle bin icon on the Windows desktop and select "delete all" to empty the bin.

On the Mac you can empty the trashcan later by clicking on it and selecting "Empty".

Permanently Deleting Files From Your Computer

When you delete a file or data from your computer, all that is deleted is the reference to it. If the space it occupied on your hard disk is then needed for new data, that space is overwritten.

Until that happens though, the earlier data is still there and it can easily be recovered using special software. As a result, it's essential that, if you want to properly delete files and information, you need to use special software that doesn't just delete the address of the data but instantly overwrites it with rubbish.

There are many programs you can buy to do this both for Windows PC's and the Apple Mac. Go onto the Internet and search for "disk wipe" to see the many on offer. A popular one for Windows PC's is www.east-tec.com .

The Apple Mac will do this for you. Select "go to" from the desktop tool bar, select "utilities" and "disk utility" and then you will see the options to delete securely.

Chapter 5 – Organise Your Computer

Recovering Old Files

On Windows XP there is no special feature to help you. If you have been taking regular back up copies of your work, you can search these to find an old file to reload and reuse. There is more detail on backup later in this chapter.

Windows Vista is a marked improvement here. Just click on the Windows icon at the bottom left corner of the screen and select "backup and restore center" from the pop-up menu. Just follow the onscreen instructions.

The Mac computer running the OSX Leopard operating system has a feature called "time machine". All the time you are using the Mac, copies of files and programs are automatically being written to an external hard disk plugged into the computer.

Let's say you are writing a book and updating, deleting and adding to it every day. Then one day, you realise you deleted a chapter by mistake a month ago. No problem.

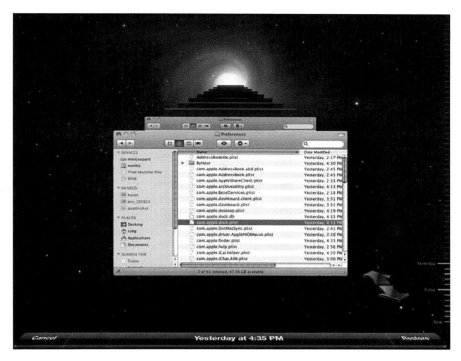

Click on the time machine icon on the dock at the bottom of the desktop and you can go back in time to recover a copy of the book as it was on any given day and restore it to use again! Of course this copy will not contain any changes made beyond the date it was saved.

Finding Files

Your hard disk will contain thousands of files and it's easy to misplace some or forget where they are stored. To save you time and frustration, Window Vista has a clever tool to help you.

There is a search box at the top right of every folder. Simply start typing what you are looking for and Windows will instantly start showing its search results. Here I have typed in "Sussex" and 2 files were found immediately.

Windows XP is not so simple, although you can still track down lost files fairly easily. Click on START and "Find" and then enter the name and type of file you are searching for. Instead of being able to locate it instantly, it reads your hard disk from beginning to end searching for it. This takes time but can be worth it. You can speed up the search by including more information in addition to the file name. For example, is it a document or picture? If you can't remember the name, you can search for some text that appears in it.

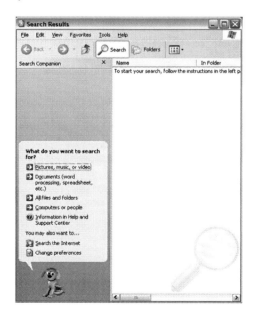

Chapter 5 – Organise Your Computer

Once again the Mac scores high on simplicity here. At the top right of the desktop toolbar is a picture of a magnifying glass. Click on this to open "spotlight". Enter what you are searching for and you can get to the files in seconds.

Safeguarding Your Files And Data

If you're like me and impatient to get going, please be sure to write this on your forehead first:

> *"FACT! One day, this computer will either die or mess up some/all of my files. I will lose my photos, letters, financial details and more and I will be as sick as a parrot! Unless I learn to take regular copies of my files and store them somewhere away from my computer!"*

And here is today's true story to ram it home. This morning I started early as usual. Up at 5:30 am and off to the gym for some exercise that everyone tells me I must get. So, having burned off a few calories, I was sitting down in the coffee shop and about to tuck into coffee and Danish (well I believe keeping the balance of calories is good!) and my phone rings.

"Mark, you'll never guess what!"

'What?"

"The main office PC won't start up and we can't access the customer database or any email!"

I managed to get back sharpish to discover this was the first totally "fatal" crash we had experienced in 7 years! Our friendly hardware expert came over and shook his head in an irritating sort of way…

…"Hmm, haven't seen one this bad for a while. Looks to me like the hard disk is corrupted and you'll have to start again".

Now, all those times over the past 7 years when I backed up came to be worth it. Although the last complete backup of this computer was a week ago, it wasn't the end of the world. In fact, we got a new PC, recovered our backup files to it and more or less carried on where we left off.

I cannot begin to tell you the effect on our business if we had no backup. Just imagine what that could mean for you.

Now, you may only be using your computer for personal use, but consider if you have downloaded and paid for music and software, and you have all your financial records, letters and personal photos on it. You really don't want to lose them.

The moral of the story is to backup everything as often as you can. The more often the better.

"Backing up" your data needs to be part of your regular routine. So, do what I do, write in your calendar to back up 1 or 2 times a month (or much more often if you are using your computer a lot!). Then you simply find the folders and files you don't want to risk losing and copy them somewhere else.

If you have organised all of your folders to be stored under the central "My Documents" or "Documents" folders, backing up is simple. By choosing to copy the documents folder, all of the folders and their contents that are inside are automatically copied.

There are plenty of ways to backup. You could put a blank CD ROM into your computer and copy files to it. Then take it out and store it safely. You could buy an extra hard disk drive in a small box, connect it to your computer and then simply copy all your files that way. Unplug it and store it away safely.

There are hard disks you plug into your computer with a single button on them marked "backup". All you need do is press the button and let it do its work for you automatically.

On my Apple Mac, I have a separate hard disk and MAC OSX does it for me using Time Machine as I work fully automatically. If I lose files or accidentally delete them I can go back in time to recover old copies on the extra hard disk.

There are even backup websites that you can pay to use. You can copy your files across the Internet to store them on another computer using this.

Chapter 5 – Organise Your Computer

I suggest you keep your backup copies in another building somewhere else as well. So if there was a fire or your computer was stolen, the backup files would not be lost. You would simply get a new computer and copy the files back onto it.

Backing Up Your Programs

It's easy to forget that there are 2 elements that need protecting. I've talked about your all-important personal files and data. The other element is the programs that you use. Some will have come with the computer, others will have been bought on a CD ROM and others may have been downloaded. There tends to be a gradual growth in the number of programs you install over time and you quickly lose track of them.

When you backup your data, you don't generally backup your software programs. Normally these have to be re-installed on your new machine so that once your backup files of data have been copied onto the new computer, you can carry on where you left off.

Thus if your computer dies on you and you have taken regular backup copies of your files and data, you will always be able to recover. At worst, you will get a new computer, re-install your programs and copy the backup data onto the new computer.

Here's the catch that can make a relatively simple process more of a nightmare though. Unless you have carefully kept the software programs to re-install, you will waste lots of time and energy trying to remember all the programs you had, where you bought them and often you may even end up having to buy them again.

The trick is to take a little time and plan ahead now. Keep all the programs you have bought on CD ROM together with manuals and a copy of the receipt and keep them in a "software store" cupboard. Make a note of all the programs that came with your computer and were already installed on it in the same place. When you buy a new computer you can make sure it comes with the same programs. Finally, you will often buy software programs on the Internet and download them over the broadband phone line to be installed on your computer. If this is the case, there's no CD ROM or printed manual to store. Every time you buy a program this way file a copy of the emails you will get telling you how to download and install the program together with any special code you needed to enter, the email receipt for the purchase together with the website and contact details of where you bought it.

So now you have both sides covered. You can easily buy a new computer, install the old programs and your data and save yourself hours if not days of misery.

What To Do When It All Goes Wrong

If your computer powers up correctly but is misbehaving in some way, you'll have the chance to take backups of your data and files and log what programs you have before you try to fix it, in case it all goes wrong.

Then it's a case of trying to identify the problem and fix it. This may be beyond your experience and you may need to contact that friendly person you made contact with when you bought the computer for help and advice. Alternatively, you may simply take it to your local computer store and have them perform some diagnostic tests on it to see if it can be fixed. If it can't then quite often the computer technician may be able to copy the entire contents of your hard disk, both data and programs, across to a new machine for you. Don't bank on it though.

More often than not, the most serious problem you will encounter will be when you turn your computer on and nothing happens, or in the process the computer tries to start up by loading Windows or OSX but can't complete it. You switch off and on a few times before it dawns on you there is going to be a serious problem and your mind races ahead trying to remember if you did your backups. If the contents of your computer are valuable or dear to you, this is when you get that horrible sick feeling in the pit of your stomach.

The problem is likely to be that data of one sort or another has become corrupted on your hard disk and the operating system program (Windows or OSX) cannot read it. Most, if not all, of your data could be safe on the hard disk, but you simply can't get at it.

To overcome this problem and get your computer going temporarily, you will be able to start up from a special CD ROM instead of the hard disk. Keep this CD ROM in your "software store". Simply place the CD ROM in the computer and turn it on.

For the **Apple Mac** simply use the CD ROM that comes containing OSX.

In **Windows XP** use the CD ROM that contains Windows XP.

In **Windows Vista** the Windows installations CD contains the files needed to start Windows. You can use Startup Repair and the other tools on the System Recovery Option menu to attempt repairs or restore data from a backup.

If you still have problems and you want to exhaust all the options before deciding to buy a new hard drive or a new computer there is a final step you can try. You will probably need an engineer to do this for you, but it is not complicated.

Open up your Windows computer and remove the hard disk. Open up another Windows computer and plug your faulty hard disk into it as an "extra" hard disk.

Chapter 5 – Organise Your Computer

Ensure both computers are running the same version of Windows. The second computer will work normally and when it is running, you can instruct Windows to check out your "extra" hard disk for errors and make corrections.

If that completes OK (it will take a few hours), replace the faulty hard disk in your own computer and see if it now works. If it does, you can breath a grateful sigh of relief. Look out for any signs of further misbehaviour though and change your computer if necessary. I have used this method successfully to get out of jail in the past!

Uninstalling Programs

With so many programs available that provide different ways of using your computer, it won't be long before you have a large number installed on your computer.

This is fine if you use them, but if not, they clutter up your computer and waste space on your hard disk.

When you install programs they often include many different files that interconnect with the operating system, and so to remove the program (uninstall) is not as simple as it seems. In fact, you can damage your operating system if you don't do this correctly.

Most software comes with instructions to install and uninstall it. For example, when you install my KAZ Typing Tutor, it places 2 programs in your "Start", "Programs" list. You click on the first to run the program. The second one I provide is called "uninstall KAZ". This automates correct removal from your computer for you. Most reputable software programs will have a similar feature.

If this isn't the case then Windows will attempt to do the job correctly for you.

Windows Vista, go to Windows icon, Control Panel, Programs and Features

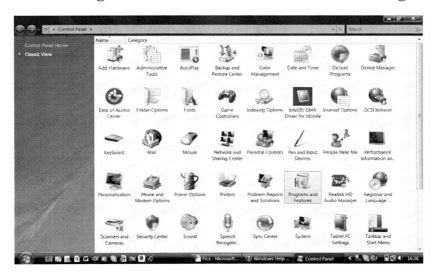

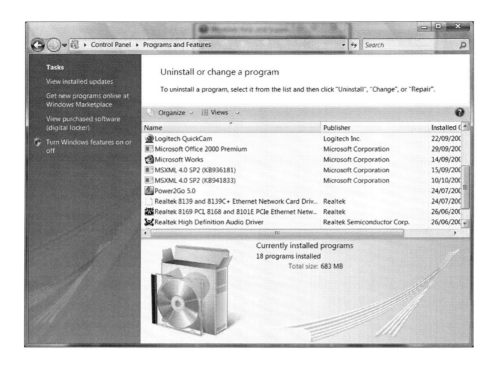

Windows XP, go to START and Control panel and select Add/Remove Programs.

Chapter 5 – Organise Your Computer 73

Things are simpler on the Mac computer. Simply click "go to" and "applications" from the desktop toolbar. Locate the program from the list. Click on it and drag it to the trash can on the dock at the bottom of the screen. If there is a shortcut to the program in the dock, click and drag it to the desktop to delete it. Job done.

Stickies

Pretty soon you'll be all over your computer. Learning new ways to do things and having fun. Then before you know it, you'll be sitting in front of your screen, wanting to repeat something you did earlier, but for the life of you, you can't remember how you did it.

Aaaarrggh!!!

Trust me, you will!

But this won't be a problem for you because the first thing you did was to make sure you had an electronic version of sticky notes running on your computer. This program comes with an Apple Mac called "Stickies" and you can get it for free for the PC as a download over the Internet at www.post-it.com. It's one of the 90 topics covered in my book, "Master Your Day" desktop organiser. You can download this e-book for free at:
http:www.kaz-type.com/freedownloads.asp

When you do something new that's not completely obvious, create a sticky note with a matching title and just type up a few words to remind you what you did.

This will save you hours of frustration and once you can remember the task and no longer need the sticky note, just delete it.

CHAPTER 6

Discover What The Internet Is, How To Get On It, Protect Your Computer And Have Some Fun

How The Internet Works

Organisations, companies and individuals by the million create websites and they want people to visit their websites, whether it's to sell something or just provide information. The Internet is simply the way all these computers can access each other.

What Is A Website?

A website is a collection of web pages stored under a web address e.g. the BBC's website is a collection of thousands of web pages and can be found at the web address www.bbc.co.uk.

When you are looking at the website you see one web page at a time. When you first go to the website, you arrive at the "home" page. This is always the same page and acts as a gateway to the rest of the website. It will consist of lots of text and pictures and have links that you click on that take you to other pages on the website or other external websites on the Internet.

You generally read what interests you on the home page and see a mention of something that takes your eye and that has a link. You click on the link and then the home page is replaced and you would then be looking at the new web page with the information that interested you. This is called "navigating" around the website.

For example, if you go to the BBC's home page at www.bbc.co.uk and look around you will see links to lots of other areas of the BBC service. You just click on the one that you want to be taken to. Then you can click on more links that interest you on that page and so on.

You can retrace your steps by clicking on the back arrow in the tool bar to go back one screen at a time. Normally, there will be a link on all pages marked "home" to take you straight back to the home page.

What Is A Web Page?

A web page is a document typically written in HTML (Hyper Text Markup Language). An extract of some of the HTML code used to create one of my websites would look like this:

```
<td width="527" rowspan="2" valign="top"><h1 align="left">Learn To Type </h1>
        <h1 align="left">Faster Than You Ever Thought Possible!</h1>
        <table width="100%" border="0" align="center">
        <tr>
                <td width="140" valign="middle"><table width="100%" height="100%" border="0" cellpadding="5" class="dashed">
                <tr>
```

Chapter 6 – The Internet Explained

*<td><p align="center"><img src="media/logo-computeractive.gif" width="100" height="34" />
*
<img src="media/star_yellow.gif" width="16" height="16" /><img src="media/star_yellow.gif" width="16" height="16" /><span class="style29"><img src="media/star_yellow.gif" width="16" height="16"

And the web page that the above code produces would look like this:

Don't panic! Very few people need to understand how to write web pages using HTML. Fortunately there are special programs that do it for us.

People design websites on PCs and Macs. Just as you use a program like Word to type say a letter, you use another program specially designed to help you create a website. This gives you a blank page and allows you to type in the text, import the pictures and type in links. You set the page like you would a poster.

These programs then automatically convert your designs into HTML for you. Normally you wouldn't even be aware or need to get into HTML at all, but it will help you understand how it all works.

Your HTML website is then made available on the Internet and when someone goes there using their browser program, this reads the HTML code and converts it all back into a pretty web page of text, pictures and links without anyone being aware.

There are many programs available to create web pages with. Microsoft has one called "FrontPage". A popular one is called "Dreamweaver" (http://www.adobe.com/products/dreamweaver/).

It's quite expensive and there are plenty of alternatives. Enter "website software" in your search engine to get the latest. These will include http://www.coffeecup.com, http://www.citymax.com. There are websites that provide comparisons and one of these is:
http://website-creation-software-review.toptenreviews.com/

Some of the website creation programs will also run on the Mac. However, if you use a Mac it's better to get one that is specifically designed for it. I sometimes use an inexpensive one called Rapid Weaver available from
http://www.realmacsoftware.com/rapidweaver/

What The Internet Looks Like

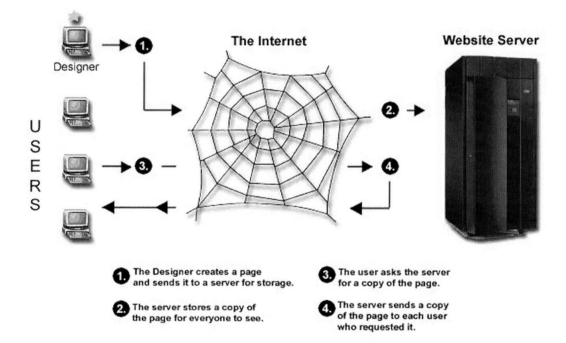

1. The Designer creates a page and sends it to a server for storage.
2. The server stores a copy of the page for everyone to see.
3. The user asks the server for a copy of the page.
4. The server sends a copy of the page to each user who requested it.

So in order to get a website "on the Internet", you have to give it an address for people to enter into their web browser so it can be located. This is called a "URL" (Uniform Resource Locator).

You see them all the time. E.g. http://www.bbc.co.uk, http://www.kaz.co.uk, http://www.amazon.com, http//ww.eBay.co.uk.

Each URL is made up of several parts.

"http" means Hypertext Transfer Protocol. This identifies the site as being available on the Internet. You normally see this, but don't need to type it into a site address. It will be done for you.

Chapter 6 – The Internet Explained

The "www" simply stands for "world wide web".

Followed by the name of the site. For example, "BBC" or "KAZ"

Then lastly the "domain extension". This denotes the type of site and where the site originates. For example ".co.uk" says the website comes from the UK. ".com" means "company" but is more often used for USA websites. ".NZ" is New Zealand. ".EU", the European Union. ".edu" means education. ".gov.uk" means the UK Government. There are many, many domain extensions, but this will give you some idea about them.

When you type in a web address, most browser programs will allow you to leave off the "http://www".

The person who created the website sitting on her PC or Mac applies to a registration service for a unique name, "kaz.co.uk" for example. If no one else is using that name then it's OK, otherwise they will have to think of an alternative name. You can register domain names at lots of websites. I use www.easily.co.uk as one of my providers. At the last count I had around 200 web domains registered. If you are going to do anything remotely to do with business on the Internet, it's a good idea to register the name before someone else does.

So people need to "plug in" their website from their computer to the Internet. When you enter a website and look it up, you can access it 24 hours a day, 365 days a year. Now it isn't practical to hook your own computer into the Internet to do this. Your computer is not always "on" and your connection speed may be poor. So websites are "hosted" on central computers that are on 24 hours a day, every day of the year on fast speed access.

So when the website has been created on a computer at home, work or school, people apply for a "hosting account" with an Internet Service Provider (ISP) who will have many computers (called servers as they serve up websites to the Internet) full of people's websites. In fact this could be hundreds of computers sometimes called a "server farm".

These computers are often physically located near the main "backbone" cabling that connects computers around the world. So every website they have on them (that they host) will deliver their content across the Internet as fast as possible, 24 hours, 365 days a year. The person then copies their website they created on the PC or Mac over the Internet and onto the ISP server computer.

Now when anyone from anywhere in the world types in the website address, e.g. www.kaz-type.com, they will immediately be taken to the copy of the website they created that is on the ISP computer.

Each time the website is changed, it is "uploaded" to the ISP's server for anyone on the Internet to access.

Large companies employ teams of specialists to produce websites, including designers, programmers and more. For most small websites, it's more common for 1 person to design, create and keep the website updated. This person is normally called the "webmaster".

Don't get hung up on this though. All you do is enter a web address like www.bbc.co.uk and you get to see its contents straight away.

Getting On The Internet

All the majority of people want is to be able to connect to the Internet from their personal computer and start to "surf" around websites and send email (more later).

You need an account with an Internet Service Provider. This will be a company with lots of central computers that access the millions of websites very quickly and send them down your phone line so you can see them on your computer screen.

They will normally offer different types of Internet access and account. The fastest access to the Internet is called "Broadband" and is very common. There are slower types of access called "dial up", which frankly are painfully slow to use. You can waste hours waiting for large files like pictures to download over your phone line and appear on your screen.

The benefits of broadband are much faster access to the Internet and downloading files plus it doesn't tie up your telephone line. You can still use the phone when you are on the Internet on your computer.

The market for broadband is very competitive and you should shop around. You will see providers using speed of access to the Internet to attract you. A fast speed currently is 8Mbps but the average is more like 4Mbps. This is the speed at which data comes down the phone line and onto your computer. If you are loading a web page with lots of pictures you will have to wait longer for it to load if you have a slow connection. Generally, the further you are away from your local telephone exchange, the slower your connection.

An invisible complication is that homes in your area may use the same Internet Service Provider's broadband through the same telephone exchange sharing the access. The more homes sharing the slower your access will be. You will notice this at peak surfing times in the evenings between 6pm and 11pm.

Your access speed can also be slowed if there are several family members accessing the Internet at the same time sharing the broadband connection.

Most people are very happy with their broadband access. Ask your phone company if they offer Internet Access Accounts and then speak to everyone you know using broadband for their recommendations.

Mobile Broadband

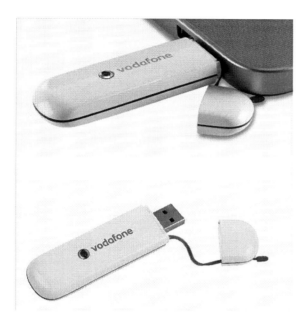

If you have a laptop computer there is an alternative to using wireless hotspots (see separate section).

A USB device connects to your laptop and gets you online via the mobile telephone network. It's not yet as good as the fixed telephone line access you have at home, but it's improving all the time. You would use this whenever you are on the move, perhaps on the train or anywhere else you want to use your laptop and go online.

Costs vary and there is normally a monthly charge for the service. Check what if any limits on access there are since more and more videos and audio files are available on the Internet and these use more bandwidth.

Most of the major telephone companies are now offering mobile broadband access packages.

Email

I will be telling you all about email in the next chapter, but it's important to realise at this stage that there are 2 types of email service to choose from.

1	Web-based free email services like www.gmail.com are accessed using your web browser to log into their website to send and receive email.

2   Dedicated paid for email services that operate separately from your normal Internet access. These email server computers only handle email and not websites, have no adverts and require a special program to make use of them called an "email client".

If you want to access your email messages from any computer anywhere in the world that has Internet access, you need do nothing more as you can access free email from email websites.

BUT if you are spending most of your time at a single computer at home, running a business or you want a more personal email address, then you should buy this from your Internet Service Provider at the same time. In fact, many give you both for the same price.

Internet Security

As Windows PC's are much more widely used, they tend to suffer from all of the security problems you hear about in the news. You will need to install software and buy services to protect yourself.

If you run an Apple Mac then the picture is very different. I've run a Mac for 5 years, have not needed to take any extra protection and have not experienced any security problems.

That's not to say you wouldn't as well, but typically Apple Macs are more secure than Windows PC's.

So this section is mostly about your Windows PC. Regardless of the version of Windows you are using, there are thousands of people intent on "hacking" your computer one way or another over the Internet. I have read that every 12 minutes you are connected to the Internet an attempt may be made to "hack" your computer.

So you need to be on your guard at all times when you are using the Internet or email. Criminals work full time on stealing identities, credit card details and more.

So here are some names to scare you: Viruses, Worms, Trojans, Key Loggers, Bots and so on. Sounds like the cast of an episode of Doctor Who!

Imagine some charming and very bright people who do nothing all day but produce programs to steal identities, credit card details, destroy data. Don't you just love 'em!

Don't fret though, just get some standard protection software that will block them from accessing your computer over the Internet and then learn some common sense rules when using the Internet and email.

Chapter 6 – The Internet Explained

If you are reasonably "savvy" you should be fine. My tips for security include the following:

1. If you are shopping online, try to use only recognised or recommended websites.
2. Don't fill in forms on the Internet that ask for personal information unless you are certain the website is reputable.
3. When you are entering sensitive information, look at the web address. If it begins with HTTPS:// it's secure. If it is just HTTP:// then it is non-secure.
4. Make sure the page you are filling in with your credit card details has a security lock on it. That's normally a small picture (icon) of a padlock somewhere at the top or bottom edge of the screen. This indicates your data will be encrypted and kept secure when it is sent over the Internet. If you don't see the padlock, don't use the site to buy online. Try calling and placing your order on the phone instead.
5. Never use a debit card because if you are ripped off you will have no come back.
6. Use a single credit card for purchases on the Internet. Don't use the card anywhere else. If you are ripped off, the credit card company should refund your money.
7. Don't tell your computer to remember your passwords automatically when you visit any websites. If your computer gets stolen the thief will have a field day.
8. Be aware that some unscrupulous people will set up fake websites. They simply copy the real website and then try to get you to order something and pay by credit card. If in any doubt, call them first to check.
9. Never order anything from a website that doesn't include a contact telephone number, address and company details.
10. Never open emails that look suspicious and NEVER open a file attached to an email unless you know who is sending it and it is expected. This is the most common way criminals use to attack your computer. The attachment contains a hidden program that could destroy all of your data or steal your personal details. More about email later.
11. Never reply to emails from strangers or anything that arrives unsolicited or of unknown origin.
12. Assume everything you do on the Internet and with your email is not private. Your ISP provider has to keep a record of the sites you visit by law, the police can intercept emails and they have forensic computing that attempts to recover data from hard disks that people have tried to erase.
13. Keep children safe. Use computers in communal areas of the home and teach them to beware of strangers online. Tell them not to use their real names in chat rooms and only respond to people they know. Discourage posting of video clips or photos that show what school they go to or where they live and to never give out a telephone number or address.

14	Back up all of your data as I mentioned before. If the worst happens, all you need do is copy back the data and carry on where you left off.

Anti Virus Software

Since new virus programs are on the Internet everyday, it follows that your Anti Virus software must develop to cope with them. The normal way to do this is for the program to update itself over the Internet automatically every time you connect. So you don't have to worry.

Hacking means gaining access to your computer to do various nefarious things. This could range from showing you adverts to monitoring your keystrokes looking for your passwords and, in the most extreme event, even destroying your files on your hard disk.

Buy Anti Virus software straight away. This simply installs onto your hard disk and watches over everything happening all the time. It is programmed to spot and destroy any problems, virus programs or programs that people may try to download onto your computer without you knowing. It also checks your email for security problems (more later). You'll find details of these at your local computer store or on the Internet or in my book "Master Your Day", which you can download for free at www.kaz-type.com/freedownloads.asp.

Go to your local computer store to see what the latest products are. I use MacAfee (http://www.mcafee-online.com/uk/), but there are many others. Go to one of the online free search engines like www.google.co.uk or www.ask.co.uk, enter "anti virus" into the search box to get a list. The good thing is that most of these now don't just protect you from Viruses, they cover pretty much all the other risks you can be exposed to as well.

Firewall

A "Security Firewall" is built into your Windows software. This simply means that when anyone tries anything suspicious in accessing your computer, it will block them and tell you. All you need to do is make sure it is turned on.

This will be a slightly different procedure depending on the version of Microsoft Windows you have on a PC and Mac OSX on the Apple Mac.

On your PC, go to your "Start" button, choose "help" and look up "firewall" for simple instructions on how to do this. On the Apple Mac click on "help" from the desktop toolbar and enter "firewall" for full instructions.

Chapter 6 – The Internet Explained

Wifi

If you have a Wifi (short for Wireless Fidelity) router (home hub box) in your system, you can access your computers via a "wireless" connection (see Hardware). And this means if you can access them, so can anyone else with a wireless access built into their computer. So for example, someone with a wireless laptop just needs to be sitting within range of your wireless router box, and they can also access any of your computers. There are stories of people sitting outside homes and offices in cars accessing people's computers inside.

Remember I talked about the Firewall switch you need to turn on in the Windows or MAC OSX operating system programs?

Well, just to confuse you some more, there is also a "Firewall" built into your router box. It's not a physical switch but you do need to follow the instructions that came with it. This will show you how to turn it on (enable it) via your screen and keyboard.

Now, one final thing with your WIFI Router Box. To increase your security even more and stop any unauthorised person gaining access to your computer, you can set it up to bar anyone or any computer that does not have a special password of your choosing.

If you are new to this you can simply follow the instructions that came with the Router. However, I recommend buying your computer from someone who can help you get all this set up properly. It's a bit like being faced with setting up a new hi-fi, TV and surround sound system. If you are knowledgeable or have the time and inclination to learn, read and follow the instructions you can do it yourself.

If you are like me, I am happy to pay someone who does this every day of the week, to do it for me. They will do it properly and in a fraction of the time, plus they will be a useful help contact for the future (which I guarantee you will always want and need).

Passwords

It's a good idea to set your computer up with password access so if you lose it, no one else can access your files. You can set up different password access for a number of people sharing the same computer. When each person "logs on" to use the computer, they are shown only their files and documents.

To find out how to do this on a Windows PC go to Start or the Windows icon, Control Panel and then User Accounts.

On a Mac computer click on System Preferences from the tool bar and choose "accounts" to get the low down.

You will need to come up with a password to enter every time you turn the computer on.

To complicate things, when you start using the Internet for lots of things like shopping, banking and much more, many times you will need to specify a password you want to use for security when you "log in" to lots of different websites. This is to ensure only you have access to the information and are not a criminal.

It is dangerous to use the same password everywhere. Criminals rely on this. They have special "password cracking" programs that will try to guess your password. If you think this is impossible, think again. These programs can create and try thousands of possible password combinations in seconds until they crack yours.

It's your job to prevent this so:

1. Make up a complicated, meaningless password that combines both letters and numbers. E.g. sderr1wwe4 or if you want to use a word substitute some of the letters for numbers. For example, zero for an "O", 1 for an "l". So a password based on "football" could be "f00tba11".

2. Use at least 8 characters and preferably a lot more

3. Mix upper and lower case

4. Use a different password for every website

Great advice, but unless you are memory woman, you'll forget the ones you don't use very often. So here's what you need to do:

If you use a Windows PC and have Microsoft Word, create a new file. Type in all your passwords and where they are used. Then you can save this document you have just typed with its own password.

So all you need to do is remember one password to open the document to see all the rest. Click on Help when you are in Word and search for "password protect" to see how to do this.

You can do exactly the same on an Apple Mac, or your computer may have a special program called "Vault" on it. Go to the Applications folder and have a look for it. This program works pretty much the same way, but is even more secure.

Now, of course if you lose or forget the password to open this file, you are stuffed! Chances are you will remember it as it's the only one you will need to remember.

So make a note of it and hide it away somewhere safe!

Conclusion

A good place to learn more about security on the Internet for Windows PC is www.microsoft.com/protect

None of this is normally necessary on an Apple Mac, but it is wise to check the latest information with Apple at www.apple.com/support

The important thing to remember is that finding willing people to help you as you are learning to use your computer is hard. Most people are really busy and they instinctively know that there's no such thing as a couple of minutes to fix a problem. So having someone, ready willing and able is worth his or her weight in gold. Make a personal connection with the people you are buying from and be sure to make some clear expectations of the service level you may need.

Some people describe the Internet as the Wild West and it's true that much of it is rubbish. As well as dodgy websites, the sex industry and gambling industries have discovered it's a very lucrative way to make money.

So, it's very important to get a good understanding of the risks for you and your family and take the simple but necessary precautions needed to stay safe and secure online.

The upside is, the Internet has transformed the way we live, work and play. Used wisely, it is a wonderful powerful tool that will open a whole new world of opportunities for you no matter what your age or level of computer experience.

Just remember to fasten your seatbelt before you set out! Start reading up about Internet security and get savvy quickly. You'll find more simple security and other tips, ideas and strategies to organise your computer in my free bonus e-book, "Master your Day" (www.kaz-type.com/freedownloads.asp)

CHAPTER 7

Learn The Basics Of Word Processing, Spreadsheets And Other Software Programs

Using Your Computer (Without The Internet)

There are hundreds of uses for your computer from playing games to keeping accounts to writing a letter or book. Pretty much everyone will want some core programs to use. These are the Microsoft programs. As a collection of programs they are called "Microsoft Office".

Depending on the version of Microsoft Office, the number of programs you get will vary. The 2 most popular are Microsoft Word, word processor program and Microsoft Excel spreadsheet program. Quite often these will be provided with your computer and included in the price. If not, you will need to buy them from your computer store. They come on CD ROMs and are in a boxed package.

There's no reason to stick with Microsoft for these programs because there are even free programs available that you can download over the Internet that will do much the same thing. You simply need to search on the Internet for them, which I will show you how to do further on.

There are many versions of Word and Excel going back to 1995. At the time of writing the latest release is 2007. However by far and away the largest user base is for 2003 on Windows XP. I will illustrate 2003, but whatever version you are running will contain similar features and ways of doing things. If you are ever stuck, always click on Help from the tool bar and type in the issue. The instructions are very easy to follow.

Microsoft Word Basics

If your computer doesn't come with this program, you will normally buy the CD ROM, pop it in your computer and follow the screen instructions to copy it (install it) onto your computers hard disk, ready for use.

Starting Word

On your Windows PC, move your mouse to move the cursor (pointer) on the screen to the START button on the bottom of the screen, click on the mouse and then choose "Programs". Then find Microsoft and click on "Word".

Chapter 7 - Software Basics

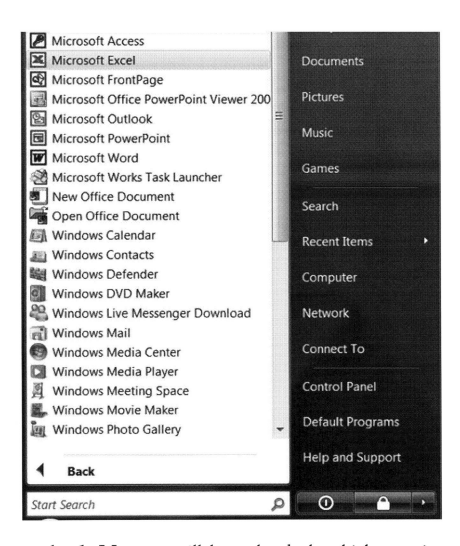

On your Apple Mac you will have the dock, which contains your most often used programs. So move your cursor to the bottom of the screen and the dock will pop up into view. Look for the big "W" picture (icon) and click on it. If it's not there, click on "Go To" at the top of the screen, select "Applications". Look down the list for Microsoft Word and click on it.

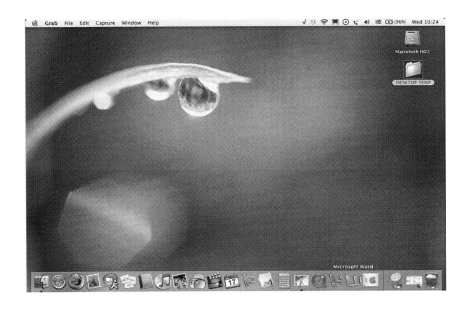

Using Word

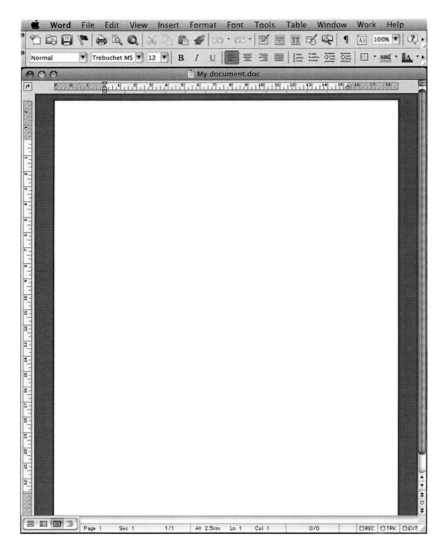

Most programs are designed to work in a similar way so the good news is once you have mastered one, the rest get quite intuitive and easy to find your way around.

At the top you have the "Menu Tool Bar" where you will find titles like, "File", "Edit", "View" etc. You go to these to do things like save or print a copy of your document, change the page layout and much more.

Move your cursor to each title and click on it and you will see that under each heading, like File, Edit and so on, a little menu of choices relating to the heading will drop down. You simply click on the one you want to use.

Underneath this you might see another tool bar, but instead of seeing titles, you see little pictures (called "icons"). This is where many of the most common tasks are represented by pictures. All you need is to click on the relevant icon to do something straight away. For example, if you click on the picture of a printer, you can print your document. If you hold your cursor over each one, a small text box should open reminding you what each picture does when you click on them.

You may see more tool bars under these. A popular one is the formatting toolbar. This allows you to change the size, type and colour of fonts you are using when you are typing and also to easily centre or justify text or indent or insert bullets and numbers.

Go to the Menu Tool Bar at the top and click on "View", then look at the dropdown menu and select "toolbars". This will give you a full list of toolbars you can have on display. You can easily turn a toolbar off and on with this selection.

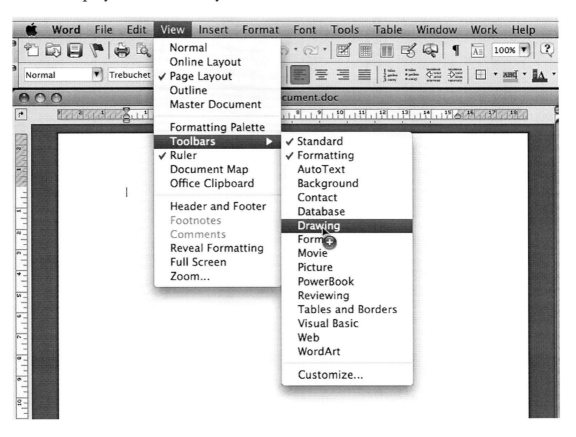

My top tip for using Word (or any other program) is to find the "Help" button. In this case it is on the Menu Tool Bar. Go here first to look up how to do things and save yourself time. Remember to make a short reminder note of how you did things and file it so you can easily look it up later to save time. Eventually, when it becomes second nature, you can delete the notes.

Create A Document

Click on "File" and then "new blank document" from the Menu bar. If you hover your mouse over the picture (icon) below of a blank page a little text box will also tell you if you click this picture you can start a new blank document. So you can see there are 2 ways to go. Clicking on the icon is quickest, with just one click.

Remember the number of functions you can perform this way is limited to the number of pictures on display though.

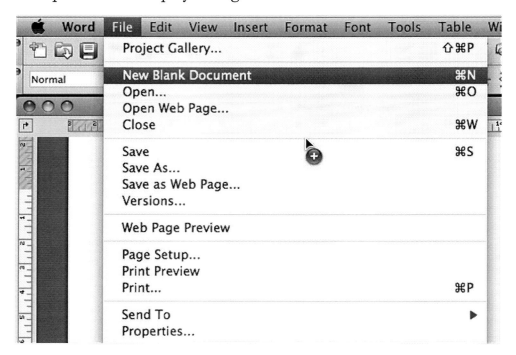

Underneath the tool bar you will see your blank page on which you can start typing. Let's do a small exercise here. Type up the following and then return when completed

Monthly Meeting

Please note that this month's meeting will be held in the church hall next Wednesday.

Well done! Now Word is showing you the font (or style of letters) that is the default. Have a look on the tool bar and if you have the formatting tool bar displayed (see earlier for how to turn this on), you will see the name of the font and the font size. Mine is showing Verdana 12, but yours will probably be different.

Chapter 7 - Software Basics 95

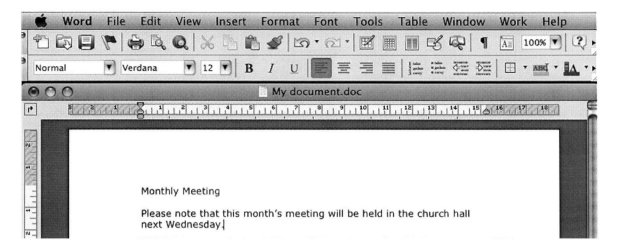

Let's change this. First the heading "Monthly Meeting" could stand out more. Place your cursor at the start of the line, click and hold down your mouse button. Now drag the cursor to the right and you will see the words are highlighted.

Now, go up to the formatting tool bar and click on the small arrow to the right of the name of the font. From the drop down menu, choose another one. Do the same with the size next to it. You can play with text this way to get all sorts of effects. Always highlight the text you wish to change first.

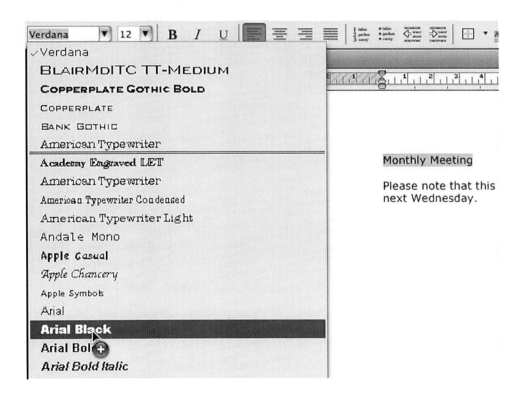

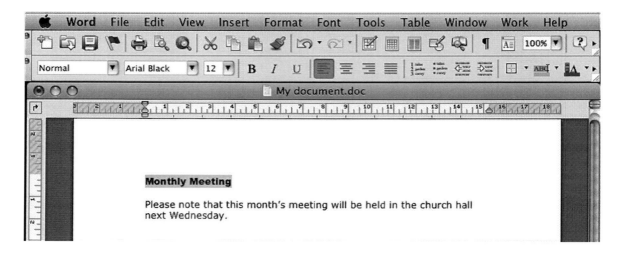

Next move the cursor to the little box next to the size marked "B" and click on it. This makes the text bold. Click it again and this turns bold off.

In the same way you can click on the "I" and "U" to make the letters italic and to underline them.

If you move right along the tool bar you'll see the letter "A" with a colour underneath it. Click on the little arrow to the right of it and you will see a choice of colours. Click on the one you like to change the letters to that colour.

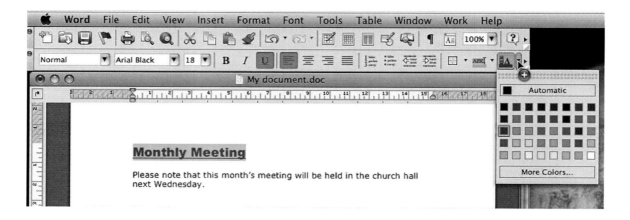

If you hover your cursor over each icon on the tool bar, it will tell you in a little box what each one does. If you want to know more about any of them, select "Help" on the top tool bar and look them up.

Save And Print

To print your document, simply click on the icon (picture) of a printer, or go to the top menu tool bar and select "File" and then select "Print" from the menu that drops down.

Chapter 7 - Software Basics

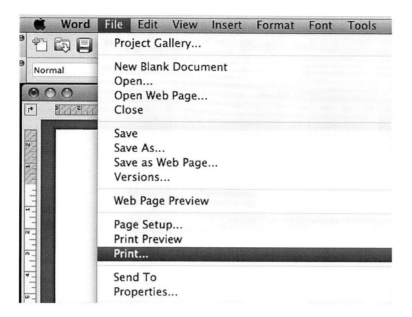

Or just click on the "print" icon.

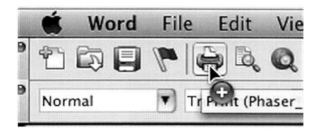

Once you close the Word program or shut your computer down, you will lose your document unless you "save" it on your hard disk. So once again this is simple. Click on the icon showing a picture of a disk or go to "File" and then select "Save As" if this is the first time you are saving the file, or "Save" when Word will simply overwrite the last version you have saved with the new one.

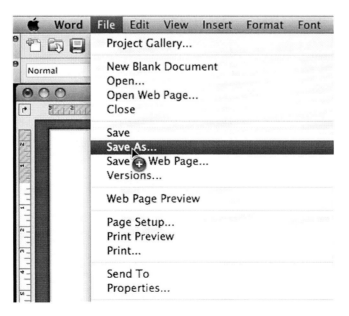

Or use:

Your computer will ask you where to save it on your hard disk. Be careful to save your document in the correct folder here. If you remember, you will have created some folders in your main "Documents" folders. Simply choose the appropriate one.

Close Word

"On a PC, go to "File" and click on "Exit" from the toolbar drop down menu. On a Mac, go to "Word" and click on "Quit Word" from the drop down menu. Alternatively you can click on the cross in the top right hand corner of your screen on a PC or top left on a Mac"

I can only touch on the basics of Word here. Please visit my website for details of self-teach courses that provide in-depth learning.

My top tip is to click on "help" and select "tip a day". Then every time you start the program, Word will introduce you to a new feature and you can learn gradually. You can also go to Microsoft's website www.microsoft.com and search for training modules.

Spreadsheets

There are many to choose from, but again Microsoft's one is the most popular. This is called "Excel". Again it may already be installed on your computer, or if not it generally comes as one of the programs in Microsoft Office as I described earlier. You install it in the same way as Word.

Chapter 7 - Software Basics

Starting Excel

On your Windows PC, move your mouse to move the cursor (pointer) on the screen to the START button on the bottom left of the screen, click on the mouse and then choose "Programs'. Then find Microsoft and click on "Excel".

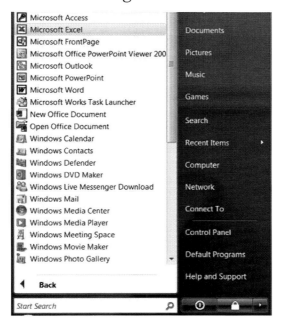

On your Apple Mac you will have the "dock" which contains your most often used programs. So move your cursor to the bottom of the screen and the dock will pop up into view. Look for the big "X" picture (icon) and click on it. If it's not there, click on "Go To" at the top of the screen, select "Applications". Look down the list for "Microsoft Excel" and click on it.

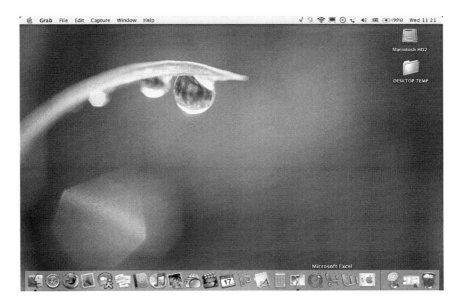

Using Excel

The main screen

The tool bars function in exactly the same way as the one in Word. Of course, some of the functions will differ as this program does a different job for you, but you get the idea.

The main screen is a grid of "cells". Along the top you see cells A,B,C,D etc. Down the side you see 1,2,3,4,5,6,7 etc.

So if you want to refer to the contents of the cell in the top left hand corner, you can see the cell reference above is "A" and the one to the left is "1". So this is cell "A1".

Chapter 7 - Software Basics

The simple way to think about this is to type a list of numbers, one in each cell under the other like this.

3
4
22
3
4
3

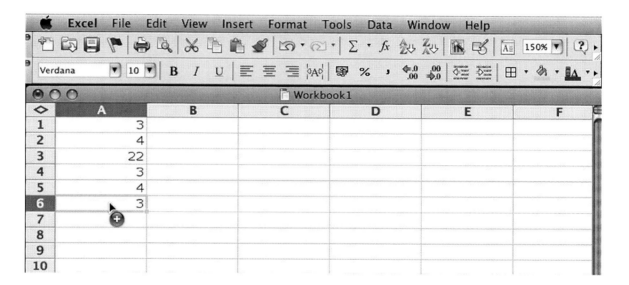

So far so easy, but now it gets clever. Ensure you have typed these numbers in and then move your cursor, click and select cell A7. This is where we want Excel to calculate the total of all the numbers above.

Now rather than you adding them up and typing the result in, we need to tell Excel that the contents of A7 will be the total of the cells A1 to A6 inclusive.

So far so good. Well you could type that calculation in like this
A1+A2+A3+A4+A5+A6 and then press Enter.
Excel will work that out and display the result for you in A7.

Or you can highlight the cell A7 and then select the "autosum" icon from the top tool bar. Hover your cursor over each icon until you find it. It looks like an "M" on its side.

Click it and it will guess what cells you want to add up for you. In this case it has suggested a formula to add the cells up for you.

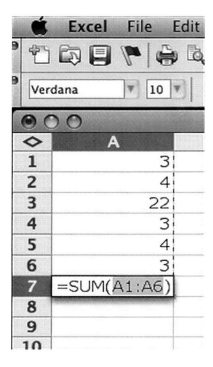

Just press Enter and, hey presto, it's done!

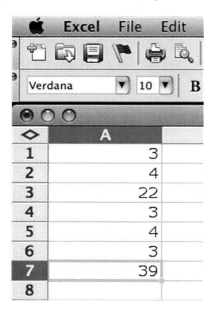

Chapter 7 - Software Basics

So now you can see you can play "what if" very easily on a spreadsheet. Let's say you were making a wooden birdcage and wanted to see how much it costs and sells for and therefore how much profit you can make. There could be many items to cost and add up to calculate the final cost.

	A	B
1	BIRD CAGE	
2		
3	MATERIALS	
4	Wood	2.45
5	Nails	0.45
6	Paint	1.2
7	Labour	10
8	Total Costs	=SUM(B4:B7)
9		
10	Sale price	
11		

You can see I have typed in the names of each cost in the "A" column and then entered the numbers in the "B" column so any cell cannot only contain numbers but can also contain headings or any words. If you look at the tool bar and hover over some of the icons you can see you can format the text in the same way you do using Word. So, for example, you could have smaller of larger text.

So now we have the costs to make the birdcage and the total cost is an automatic calculation of the list of costs in cells B4 to B7. By using the autosum feature this is done for you. Just press Enter to the suggested formula it is showing you in B8 to give you the total costs of 14.10.

	A	B
1	BIRD CAGE	
2		
3	MATERIALS	
4	Wood	2.45
5	Nails	0.45
6	Paint	1.2
7	Labour	10
8	Total Costs	14.1
9		
10	Sale price	
11		
12	Profit	

Next we can enter the amount you want to sell your birdcage for in cell B10. Let's say 29.50.

	A	B
1	BIRD CAGE	
2		
3	MATERIALS	
4	Wood	2.45
5	Nails	0.45
6	Paint	1.2
7	Labour	10
8	Total Costs	14.1
9		
10	Sale price	29.5
11		
12	Profit	

Finally, you want Excel to calculate the profit for you in cell B12. So move your cursor to B12 and type in the formula: =B10-B8 and press the Enter key. Then your profit is shown as 15.40.

	A	B
1	BIRD CAGE	
2		
3	MATERIALS	
4	Wood	2.45
5	Nails	0.45
6	Paint	1.2
7	Labour	10
8	Total Costs	14.1
9		
10	Sale price	29.5
11		
12	Profit	15.4

This is where spread sheets come in very handy. They allow you to play "what if". So when things change you get an instant picture of how the results are affected.

You have found another supplier of paint and you can reduce the price from 1.20 to 1.10. Plus you can sell it for more, let's say 32.50. Just type the new numbers into those fields and the new results appear automatically.

	A	B
1	BIRD CAGE	
2		
3	MATERIALS	
4	Wood	2.45
5	Nails	0.45
6	Paint	1.1
7	Labour	10
8	Total Costs	14
9		
10	Sale price	32.5
11		
12	Profit	18.5

Next you can save your worksheet to hard disk to preserve it in exactly the same way as you did using Microsoft Word. Just click on "Save" in the dropdown File menu, which can be found on the top tool bar.

You use exactly the same techniques to print your worksheet and close the Excel program as I've already shown you when using Word.

Now you can see how using a computer gets easier because most programs are designed to operate in a similar way.

This is a simple example of how to use a spreadsheet program. You can now begin to appreciate the power of spreadsheets and the vast number of ways in which people use them. In this example the contents of the total costs and profit cells are "relative" to each other. There is no limit to the number relative cells.

Here's a "big" use of spreadsheets. Imagine the millions of parts that go to make up a 747 aircraft. By setting up spreadsheets with the details of costs of each one, it's then automatic to see the overall costs change as new suppliers and prices come in. There can be tens of thousands of lines to the spreadsheets and they can be organised into departments and then consolidated together. A huge set up certainly, but one that will ensure efficiency in the manufacture process. Change anyone of a million parts and the cost of the 747 across all parts is instantly recalculated.

A business will use a spreadsheet to forecast what money it needs in the bank to function. This is called "Cash Flow Forecasting". A spreadsheet is created for the business that lists all the various costs from staff to premises, cost of borrowing, advertising and so on and so on. Then the estimated sales are entered together with bank balances, how long invoices take to be paid and a whole lot more.

Once completed, the business can experiment to see how much its profit and cash requirements are affected by, for example, increasing sales by 5% or reducing the number of staff, or increasing the advertising spend.

There are many simpler uses for spreadsheets at home. For example, you could use it to list a catalogue of stamps with their value to give you a total. Then when you add or sell stamps you get an instant overall valuation. Use them to do the same with stocks and shares. You could start to record you personal accounts with one. The list is endless.

Once you have set your spreadsheet up, you have created a "template". To save time, you can buy or even get other templates for free that you can use straight away or change to suit your needs. Search on the Internet for "free excel templates" and you will find many websites to choose from. A good place to start is with Microsoft at http://office.microsoft.com/templates/. Go to the bottom of the web page and look for templates for Excel.

I can only touch on the basics of Excel here. Please visit my website for details of further in-depth learning.

Using Photo Software

The good news is since so many of us use our computers to share digital photos, Microsoft Windows and Mac OSX have provided built in tools to make it much simpler.

First off though, take a few minutes to organise where you want to store your folders. Otherwise, just like a shed load of old printed photos that are all mixed up, you won't be able to easily find or use the photos when you want them.

Chapter 7 - Software Basics

Windows

Go to the Windows icon in Windows Vista and choose Pictures to get going.

In Windows XP go to the Start button and choose My Pictures. Then start creating some new empty folders to store pictures in. You can add or delete folders, or move pictures between folders later if you get it wrong.

You can right click on any folder and then select "new" and "folder" to start creating your filing system.

Mac OSX

The Apple Mac has a special program called "iPhoto" which comes with your computer. You should find it by looking along the dock at the bottom of the screen or click on "Applications" from the toolbar and then the drop down menu and click on iPhoto to start it up.

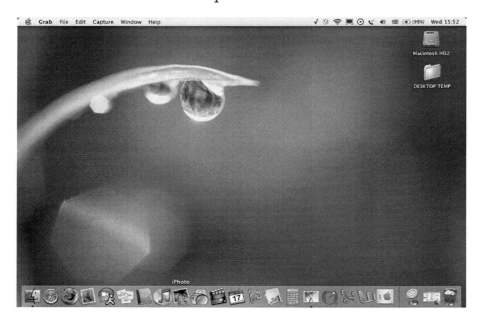

iPhoto main screen

Click on the "+" sign at the bottom left of your screen to select "new album" and then start giving them names. E.g. "Summer holiday 08", "Paul Wedding" etc.

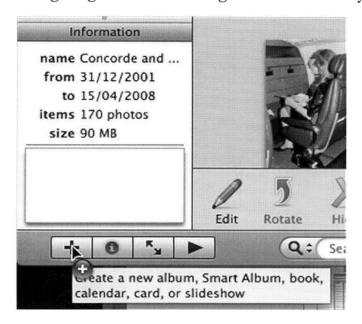

OK, now you have organised where you want your photos to be stored on your computer, next we need to get them in ("import").

Getting the photos from your camera (importing photos from a digital phone is exactly the same).

Firstly, your computer will need to recognise your camera when you connect it so before you do this, check to see if your camera may have come with a CD ROM. If so, pop it in the computer and follow the instructions. If not, don't worry, your computer is pretty smart and will almost certainly manage anyway.

You will probably have a cable with your camera that connects the camera straight into your Windows PC or Apple Mac computer. Or if your camera and computer have a "Bluetooth" wireless connection, they will simply "beam" the photos across without the need for wires. I suggest you leave that for later as it can get fiddly.

On a Windows PC a small window should appear asking what you want to do with the incoming photos and this should allow you to select one of the new folders you created previously. The photos folders will open up for you. It's as simple as that.

Windows Vista users have the Windows Photo Gallery to view and refine photos.

On an Apple Mac, the iPhoto program will automatically start up and you simply select "Import To Library" from the File drop down menu on the top tool bar. These go into the library and once there, you can highlight them and drag them into the correct folder you created earlier. These folders are listed down the left hand column.

Photo Software

If you are like me, you'll have a cupboard full of old photos plus lots more you have taken on a "digital" camera. Those taken on a digital camera work without the need for film and simply record your picture in a computer format.

Once you start messing with photos on your computer it's difficult to stop! That's because the whole experience of using them is miles better.

Once you have uploaded (copied) your photos from your camera or phone camera to your computer, you can organise them, print them, email them to friends, create an automatic slide show of them to music, have them as fixtures on your computer desktop when you switch it on, copy them (burn them) onto a CD or DVD to share or load into your TV's DVD player to view on a large screen, get them onto your IPod or music player if it has a screen, or even access from some devices like the Apple TV box, WII, Xbox or Play Station via your WIFI (wireless access) direct from your computer to your TV screen.

Whew!

And I probably haven't covered all the options either!

But please don't worry. Just start out with the basics and then learn as you go along. Don't rush and always remember to type up some basic notes on how you do things on a sticky note (see earlier section) so you can easily refer to them until it becomes automatic.

You can do some limited work on photos on your computer with the standard Windows and Mac software you have used. This may include things like rotating the picture, cropping it, getting rid of red eye and more.

However, there are plenty of programs that will do a whole lot more if you are serious about results. These will change the light, exposure, colours and much, much more. Check with your camera as if it did come with a CD ROM, then this often contains the manufacturers own photo manipulation program. Alternatively, you can buy separate ones like PhotoShop from www.adobe.com.

Whatever program you use, it will have a similar operation to the ones we have already looked at. That's all the buttons and knobs and toolbars (called the "interface") so you will be able to store and print photos in just the same way.

You can buy special photo paper for most printers to get a good finish, but you could also copy (burn) selected photos onto a CD ROM and take it to your local photo store that can print them professionally for a small charge.

The problem with printing yourself is that the cost of ink cartridges and special photo paper soon mount up. You might not fancy trekking down to Boots every time with a CD of photos for them to print for you and an alternative way to do this is online. Go to any number of websites like www.photobox.co.uk, www.truprint.co.uk or www.kodakgallery.co.uk. You pay online with your credit card and then "upload" your photos from your computer over the Internet. They will return them professionally printed in the post. Some services like www.tescoshop.com do the same but make them available for you to collect from your local participating store within the hour!

At the same time, you can have your photo put onto mugs, gifts and other items that you can buy.

There are a number of free programs (freeware) to use for basic photo manipulation. Go to www.download.com where there is a library of software and search for "photo editing" to find some. A popular one to start out with is Photofilter.

Scanning Old Photos

It's a great opportunity now to get all of your old photos onto your computer. Apart from being able to use them in all these new and exciting ways, you will be preserving them forever (provided you don't forget to back up your computer!).

Now, if you remember I explained that many standard "inkjet" printers also double as scanners. This means you place your photo in the machine, select "scan" from your computer or the printer and a copy is saved onto your computer. You can usually tell the computer which folder to put it in before you scan.

Digital photography is a huge topic and once you have mastered the basics, have a look on the Internet for more books and courses that will gradually increase your skill level.

Managing Your Pictures

On the Apple Mac, this is done for you and photos are automatically stored using the iPhoto program. As well as enabling you to organise your library into sections, this program also has some basic photo manipulation features.

On Windows PC's the pictures are normally automatically stored in a folder named "My Pictures" which in turn is stored with other folders in the main folder named "My Documents".

A really neat tool to manage your photo library comes free from Google. It is called Picasa and is freely available from http://picasa.google.com/

Video

This is one area where you really can have fun using your computer.

Chapter 7 - Software Basics 113

There are dozens of digital video cameras to choose from depending on what you want to use one for. They all connect to your computer so that you can edit your movies into polished productions.

When choosing a video camera, try to select one that takes High Definition movies because you will love the clarity when viewing it on a larger TV screen. I have cameras that are midsize and record footage onto tape cassettes as well as a pocket camera that records straight onto a memory card.

I work with video to produce DVD products from my home office, to produce short video clips for some of my websites and then some lo-resolution videos just for fun.

Once you have taken your video, it's the same process to import your video clips as with photos. The only difference here is they are "movie" clips you are importing to your computer.

To import, manipulate and store videos, Windows XP users can buy the Windows Media Center program, but this program comes built in with Windows Vista.

Windows Media Center

Iphoto Stores Movies On The Apple Mac

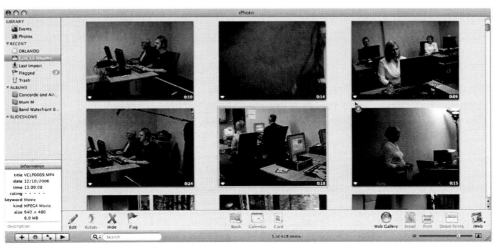

As with your still digital camera, connecting your digital video camera will automatically start up the iPhoto program for you. You select "import Photos" again and iPhoto stores each of your video clips just as it would a single photo. Except when you click on them you will see the movie play for you. You can tell the difference between a still photo and a movie clip as the movie clip includes a tiny picture icon of a video camera on the picture.

Making Movies

Editing your movies has never been simpler. Once you have imported your movie clips from your camera, the movie programs enable you to edit them, stitch them together, add music and titles plus a whole lot more. Then simply choose to Export your movie and you can put it onto DVD or save it as a file to email if it's not too large.

Hey presto! Pretty soon you can start up in business as your local wedding video photographer!

Each of these programs has a built in tutorial that can be accessed from the usual Help function. It should take you a few hours to get to grips with the basics, but once you have the skills you'll be able to produce videos very quickly in future.

Windows Vista includes the Windows Movie Maker program.

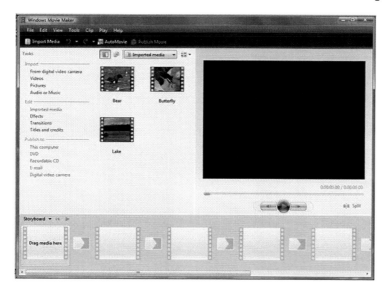

Apple Mac users get the iMovie program included. If you want to move to a professional system, consider Apple's Final Cut Studio but be prepared to spend a long time getting to grips with it.

Conclusion

There are thousands of programs available to put your computer to many different uses. Think of something you would like to do, then enter it into your Internet search engine on your Web Browser program like Google, and you will be amazed! There is more information in the following section.

Start slow and don't try and learn too much at one time as you will get frustrated. Keep your friendly "expert" contact details from when you bought the computer to hand. BUT only call them when you have tried everything yourself. If you call at the drop of a hat, this friendly support is likely to become otherwise engaged when you want them!

Type up short reminder notes all the time and get into the habit of taking a regular backup so you can feel smug if your computer eventually crashes and you will have lost nothing.

CHAPTER 8

Discover How To Surf The Internet, Enjoy Safe Shopping, Meet Family And Friends Online, Email And More

Using Your Computer On The Internet

So, congratulations! You've got your computer set up, organised your folders and mastered some of the basic software you are likely to be using.

But, let's face it, the real attraction is "getting on the Internet", "surfing the web", "going online" or whatever else you want to call it.

Getting Connected To The Internet

The wondrous content available on the Internet will be delivered down your phone line to your computer from an "Internet Service Provider" (ISP). There are millions of websites for you to look at and they are all channelled through computers (servers) owned and operated by your ISP. This is normally your phone company, but there are dozens of companies to choose from. Some popular ones are BT (www.bt.com), Virgin (www.virginmedia.com), Orange (www.broadbando2.co.uk) and Tiscali (www.tiscali.co.uk).

So, first things first, you need to open an account with an ISP. They will usually then send you a CD ROM containing a program (software) for you to copy (install) to your computer. This enables your computer to automatically dial the telephone number of your ISP and connect automatically to their Internet computer every time you start your browser program.

I mentioned Internet software earlier and talked about a "browser" program. This will almost certainly come as part of the computer. The most common is called Microsoft Internet Explorer for the PC and Safari for the Mac.

The thing to remember is once you have installed your ISP's software, you don't need to do anymore.

Then just click and start your browser and you are instantly on the Internet. All the clever stuff of connection has been taken care of for you.

The things to consider when you get your ISP are:

1. Don't always go for price. Cheaper service often means poor or expensive support costs when you need to phone them.
2. Ask your contacts to recommend an ISP they use.
3. Privacy. I look upon my ISP as providing my Internet access in the same way I see my electric or water company providing me with power and water. Therefore I would never use an ISP that analysed or kept records of my Internet activity, regardless of how reasonable they may try to make this sound. So always ask the question before deciding which one to go with.

Chapter 8 – Using the Internet

4   There are 2 types of access you are interested in. Internet and email. Both are handled by the same equipment but may be charged for separately. Check your ISP provides an email service you can use.

5   If you only want occasional use of email for personal and not business use, you could just buy Internet access, as there are free email services you can use later on the Internet, like Yahoo Mail, Google Mail and others.

6   Decide what type of connection you want. "Broadband" means fast connection and "Dial Up" means a slow connection. Both come down a telephone line in the same way. Always go for Broadband if you can afford it. 10 minutes trying to download stuff on a dial up connection and you can lose the will to live!

7   As well as providing a CD ROM with the connection program on it, you may also receive a modem. This goes between the phone cable and your computer. Check beforehand as your computer may have one already built in that you can use.

8   If you want to go "wireless" with a Wi-Fi network, they will often provide you with a free router box (home hub).

9   If you are worried about all of this coming together, it really is quite straightforward but, again, always try to have a friendly computer buff available to call if you get into trouble. The whole connection thing should take about 20 minutes if all goes well.

I've mentioned this before, but I can't stress it highly enough…

…please WAIT! Now you have got your ISP organised, just remember, it is estimated that all it takes is 12 seconds from when you connect to the Internet for your computer to be accessed by people or programs you would rather not come across.

So, this is where you have to make sure you have taken the security precautions needed to protect yourself BEFORE you start surfing the web. If you're happy to have a go there is plenty of help and advice on this topic and I included security tips in the KAZ "Master Your Day" desktop organiser e-book (that's a book you read on your computer instead of a printed book) at www.kaz-type.com/freedownloads.asp.

As I mentioned before, I use an Apple Mac and a Windows PC. This is not because I want to but because I write about both and need to use both. I have all the security tools I will tell you about installed on my Windows PC. However, currently I don't need any of them on my Apple Mac as it is not prone to the same level of security attacks. I'm sure in time this will change, but it's one of the reasons I prefer the Apple Mac.

It's quite simple really and it's worth mentioning again. There are "switches" inside your computer called Firewalls provided by Windows. You just need to check these are turned on. The same goes on your "router" if you have one. That's the external box that allows you to use computers over a wireless network. For example, you may use a laptop computer in your bedroom that is connected wirelessly to a desktop computer and a printer in the home office. Then you need to buy software to protect it all from viruses and other harmful programs and make sure you keep it up to date. Job done!

Remember too, that since you take regular copies (backup) of your important files, even if you have problems you will be able to recover OK

If you are not sure how best to protect your computer on the Internet, refer to the earlier security section again.

Everyday Internet Use

Using An Internet Browser Program

The most widely used program for the PC is Microsoft Internet Explorer and it is normally supplied with your computer. The Apple Mac comes with its own browser program called Safari. There are alternatives to both of these that you can find if you look for "free browser" on the Internet. These include 'Firefox' and Google's 'Chrome' browser.'

Most browser programs work in much the same way. The best way to find out how to use each one is to select the help function. They will normally contain simple lessons plus you can type in a question to search for specific answers.

Start your browser program the same way you started Word and Excel.

Windows Explorer Browser Program

Apple Mac Safari Browser Program

Using your browser program enables you to "navigate" or "surf" your way around millions of websites all over the world. Towards the top of the page is a box containing the Internet (web) address of the website being displayed for you.

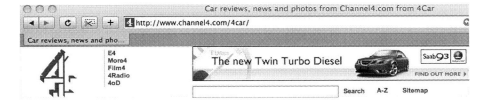

To quickly see how to go to a specific website, highlight and delete the address that is currently being displayed and replace it with www.bbc.co.uk and press enter. You are immediately whisked off to the BBC website. Now have a look at the web page and you will see lots of headings. All you do is click on one of these and the BBC will take you to the corresponding page on their website to view it.

Now look at the tool bar and you will see a back button or arrow. If you click these you can move back and forwards to revisit the pages again. If you move along the tool bar, you will see icons and choices that allow you to print the current web page, email it to someone, reload the page and more. Experiment with these until you are familiar with them.

History

Generally your computer will keep an internal record of all of your Internet activity. You can go to the tool bar and select "history" and get to see a list of all the web pages you have visited. You can simply click on any one of them to go back and see it again.

Cache

All this history is stored on your hard disk in what is called "cache". The purpose is to speed up the Internet for you. When you first visit a website a copy of the page is stored in the cache on your computer. The next time you go there, if the computer sees there is already a copy of this on your hard disk, it can load it immediately. Whereas having to download all the text and pictures from the website can take time.

You can empty this cache manually any time you want so the record of activity is deleted.

In Windows Explorer select Delete Browsing History from the tools menu.

Chapter 8 – Using the Internet 123

In Safari, click on Safari and Empty Cache.

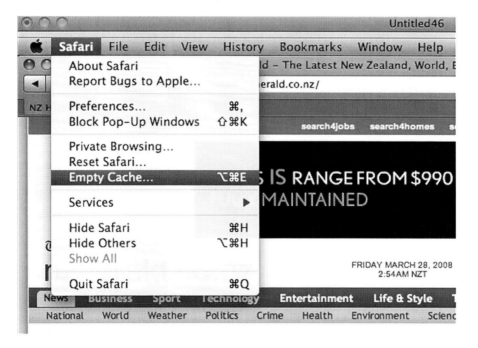

Bookmarks Or Favourites

With so many websites to see, you can quickly get lost and forget the good ones. So when you are looking at a website that you think you many want to use again, simply go to the tool bar and select "bookmarks" or sometimes they are called "favourites". This will store the address for you so that when you need it again you simply look at bookmarks to see the list and click on the one you want.

Windows Internet Explorer

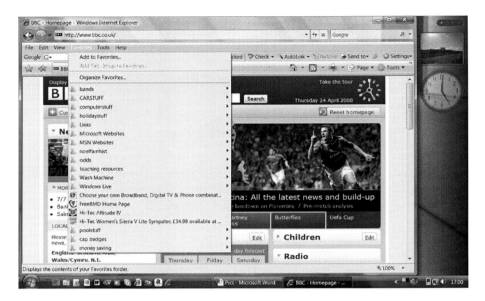

Safari Browser

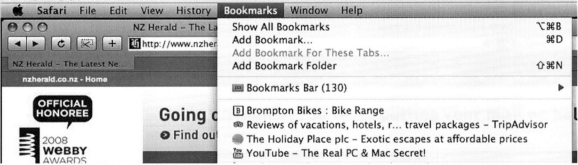

Home Page

When you run the browser program, this first web address is always the same to start with. It is called your "home" page that you always like to start out from. You can make this any page you want. So, for example, I like to have my home page as the BBC news website. So I change the settings in the browser to point to www.bbc.co.uk every time it starts up.

To change your home page:

Windows Internet Explorer

Choose Tools, then Internet Options.

Chapter 8 – Using the Internet 125

Then select the General tab and type in the web address you would like to be your home page and click on Apply.

Safari Browser Program

Click on Safari and Preferences from the tool bar and then enter your home page website in the General Tab.

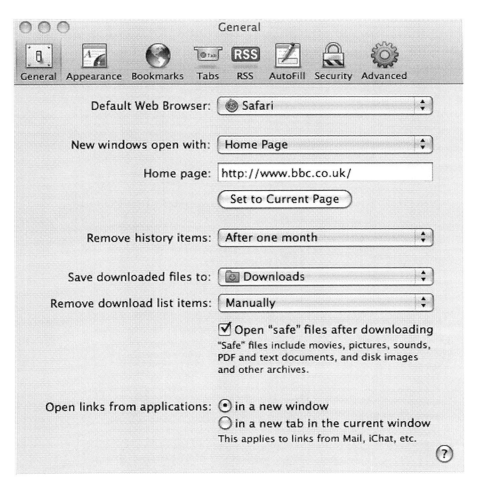

You will also find a button on the browser called the home button (often it has a small icon picture of a house). If you click on this button anytime it will always take you back to your set home page.

Print A Web Page

Quite often you will come across information on a website you would like to keep. Just like the earlier programs, you simply go to the tools bar and select "File" and then "Print".

Save A Web Page

Or you could simply save a copy of the web page to your hard disk by selecting "File" and then "Save".

Email To A Friend

There are many times that you will come across web pages you want to tell your friends about. Select File and then you can normally choose to email them the contents of the page or, if it is a big page, email them the address of the page. In that case, they get a live link in their email and all they have to do is click on it and they will be taken to the page on the Internet.

Searching On The Internet

This is the real magic of the Internet. If you think there are millions of websites sitting on computers (servers) all over the world. Each computer has an individual address and each website on them has a unique name. They are all connected via cables, wires, satellites etc. in one way or another. Just like you can connect to any phone on the planet, you can connect to any website on the planet.

With so much information stored on all these websites, you would never know how to find the stuff you are looking for in billions of web pages.

So, along came "search engines". These are free programs you run in your browser program when you are connected to the Internet. The companies that operate the search engines have buildings with hundreds and thousands of computers in them. They have programs that go out onto the Internet to each and every website. They look at each word and each page of every website and catalogue them. This is a mammoth task that is going on all the time. They store the catalogue on their computers.

Chapter 8 – Using the Internet 127

So when you are searching for something on the Internet, you will enter the website address of a search engine, e.g. www.google.co.uk, or you may even see a separate search box on your browser.

Type in what you are looking for and the search company will search their catalogue of billions of entries in seconds and give you suggested websites where you may find what you are looking for.

In this example I'm using Google at www.google.co.uk. I've typed in KAZ Typing Tutor into the search box.

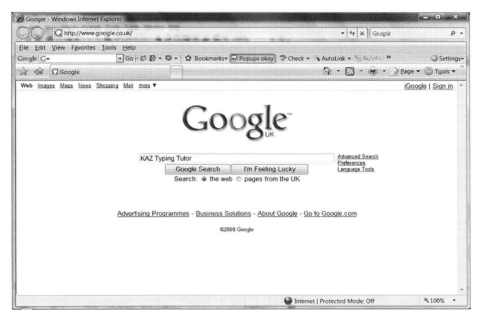

Within a second Google has searched it's database and returned theses results.

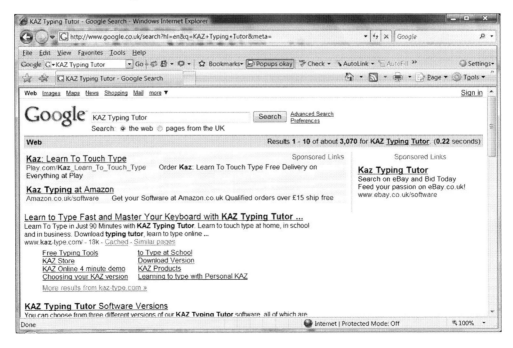

Then I simply click on one of the results to view the KAZ website.

However just typing in a single word is unlikely to give you exactly what you are looking for. For example, if I am interested in an LCD TV, if I type in TV I will get a list of websites with TV in them. However if I type in, LCD TV I will only get websites where that shows up. This can still lead to lots of pages being found that are not useful.

To really pin down your search use inverted commas. These define exact phrases and the search engine will only look for web pages that contain the exact words or phrase. For example searching for the word "Cars" retrieves thousands of results but searching for "Ford Smax" narrows the search right down.

You can literally spend your life searching if you are not careful. Try entering someone's name, government name, product name, holiday destination, homes for sale and on and on....

If you can't find what you are looking for on one search engine, then try another. There are plenty to choose from including www.google.co.uk, www.ask.co.uk, www.lycos.co.uk. Or simply type "search engine" into any search engine for a list of them.

Shopping Online

Shopping online saves the hassle of going to the stores, comparing prices and lugging products home. From food to books, clothes, TV's and furniture, people are increasing shopping online.

Chapter 8 – Using the Internet

Safe Shopping

If you observe a few simple rules you should be fine, even in the unlikely event the transaction goes wrong.

Keep a single credit card for all your online shopping. Don't use it for anything else. If it goes wrong you can claim from the credit card company. You can then destroy that card and get another one.

Therefore, never use a debit card to pay for online shopping as you are not protected.

Look for the secure symbol on the page where you are asked to enter your credit card details. This is normally a small padlock somewhere in the margins. If it's not there, stop and don't order online. Call them instead.

Only order from websites of names you know and trust or have been recommended to. Otherwise make sure the website contains phone and address details of how to order. Then call them up and satisfy yourself they are genuine. Criminals sometimes create professional websites with shops and accept credit card payments. People have paid thousands of pounds for items like TV's, only to see the website disappear along with their money. This is another good reason to always use a credit card and not a debit card to pay. The credit card company will often reimburse your loss.

Always print out the order form once you have completed it for your records. Normally you will also receive an email that confirms your order as well.

EBay

You can't pass shopping without a quick look at www.eBay.co.uk

Get yourself a cup of coffee and settle down and spend an hour looking at this website. There are plenty of Internet auction websites, but EBay is probably the most widely used. Go there to buy almost anything, new or second hand.

A note of caution though. The majority of sellers are reputable, but take some common-sense precautions. Click on "Safety Centre" from the bottom menu and learn how to protect yourself before you start trading.

Amazon

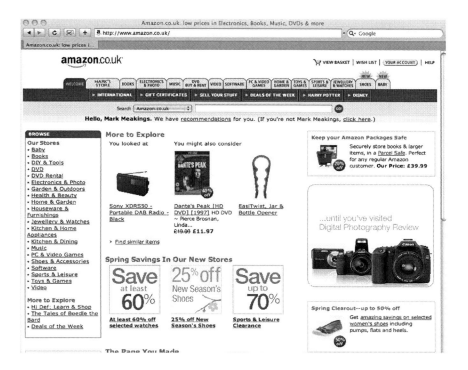

Another major Internet retailer is www.amazon.co.uk. There are plenty of them, but again this is one of the largest. Here you can buy anything from books to software and electrical items. Many famous brands are sold here. I also sell my product through Amazon and you can find it by going to www.amazon.co.uk and searching for KAZ Typing Tutor.

As Internet shopping starts to take over from shopping in stores, many more businesses are opening up online shops. These range from all the high street names you already know to companies like www.play.com and even TV shopping channels like QVC TV www.qvcuk.com

Wonders of technology, you can even watch live TV broadcast on your web browser and order items being shown at QVC. Have a look at www.qvcuk.com and click on "watch QVC Live".

Comparison Shopping

With so many websites, it can be very hard to find the best deal on products. Say you wanted to buy a new TV and knew the model. You could go to the website of the manufacturer to get details and to order it but the chances are that you'll be able to get it cheaper elsewhere.

This is where price comparison websites come in. Type "price comparison" into your search box to see some of them. You then normally enter the name of the

TV you want and the website goes to all the main suppliers and gives you a list of what they all charge!

One of the more popular ones is run by Google and is called Froogle (www.froogle.co.uk). Some others include www.pricerunner.co.uk, www.savebuckets.co.uk and dozens more.

Music

This is what most people use to enjoy their music, a digital music player.

You've probably heard of Apple's "iPod", being the most famous. This tiny device fits in your pocket. It connects to your computer with a cable that comes with the player. Using a free program called "iTunes" on the computer, you put all of your current music CD's into the computer one at a time. You can download the iTunes program for free for your Windows PC or Apple Mac from www.itunes.co.uk.

As if by magic the music gets put onto the computer. Once it is captured on the computer, it is automatically copied down the cable to the music player (synchronised). Then unplug the music player from the computer, plug in the earphones, go for a jog and listen to your music. Many cars now come with a jack to connect the music player to the car stereo system.

Finding music tracks, artists or albums in amongst thousands of songs on the computer or music player now becomes simple. You can mark your favourite music tracks and organise them into your own "play lists".

Chapter 8 – Using the Internet

For example, I've gone through my music collection and organised my music into lots of different play lists. I select these depending on the mood I am in and where I am. I have play lists called soul, top oldies, country, dinner party background, driving and lots more. A music track can appear in any number of play lists. Finally, there's a great feature to "shuffle" music. The player will just flit around your music collection playing tracks at random.

So, you can see the technology brings a whole new level of enjoyment in listening to music.

Now, I hear you cry, "I've got 500 CD's, it'll take a year to load each one onto my computer and for them to play and be recorded on the computer!"

The good news is when the computer reads your music CD to be stored, it does it many times faster that normal playing speed. On my computer this is often 16 times normal speed so it really doesn't take that long. I kept a pile at the side of my computer and just swapped CD's in and out as I worked on other tasks, so it was painless.

You can connect your computer over the Internet to online music stores, where you can buy new music with your credit card. This comes down the phone line onto the computer and then onto the digital music player that is plugged into the computer.

If you use the iTunes program you will see the iTunes Store button. Click on this to connect over the Internet to their store and search or browse for music to download and buy.

The world of music is constantly changing. The iPod currently has the lion's share of the market for music players. When you download music from the Apple iTunes online store, they place a security marker on it. This prevents you from copying it to anything other than an iPod. You can also buy music for your iPod from other online music shops. Consider Napster (www.napster.com) and Tesco (www.tescodownloads.com).

The other format for music is called MP3. Players that use music in this format don't have any restrictions and are generally cheaper than iPods.

There are hundreds of websites where you can purchase and download music in the mp3 format. Type in "mp3 music" into your Internet search box to start looking. You can import mp3 format music files into your iTunes program if you want.

It's worth mentioning here that if you have a treasured collection of old "vinyl" records, you can copy these onto your computer and enjoy listening to them with your new digital music.

There are record decks that play the records with the old arm, revolving turntable and needle and through a USB connection to the computer, convert and store them in digital format.

Sounds great, but it's often very fiddly and you get the scratches included. You might find it cheaper and quicker just to re-purchase the albums from an online music shop and be done with it.

Don't worry! It is really simple when you know how and you will love the new ways you can listen to your music. A single digital music player will hold up to 20,000 tracks and more and you can ditch the CD's or store them away altogether.

Social Networking

Nowadays anyone can be a star on the Internet! There are plenty of social networking sites to use. These started out mainly used by school children but now pretty much everyone uses them. Once you start using them, you'll wonder how you managed before.

Websites like www.facebook.com and www.myspace.com are free to use and allow you to set up your personal profile on their website. Then you can show this to friends and see theirs as well. Then you can chat to each other at the same time. This is becoming more popular than email for a lot of people.

This growing phenomenon is no longer limited to kids and 10's of thousands of 50 plus individuals frequent SagaZone (www.sagazone.co.uk).

Spend some time looking around the websites, but one word of caution. Once you create a profile of yourself, it's available for anyone to see from your Mum to your employer! So be careful.

A relatively new social website is www.twitter.com. This allows people to fire off very short messages to each other and it's catching on.

Virtual Life

The next step in social networking is "virtual" networking where you go to a website and get to wander around a virtual world and the terrain in order to meet and interact with other people through "alter egos".

There are various virtual world websites including http://secondlife.com/ and www.activeworlds.com. www.there.com is rated PG13 has no adult content. For the young ones try www.clubpenguin.com.

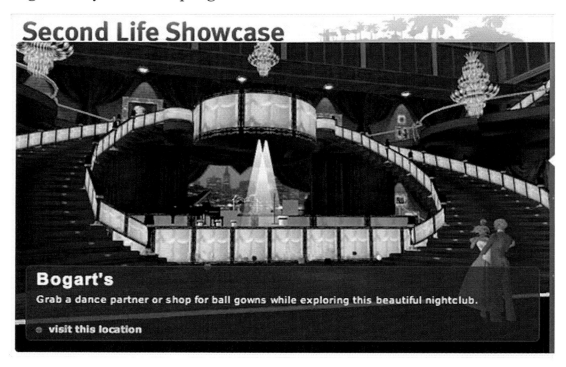

You create an "avatar", an online representation of yourself, and this is how other people "see" you in the virtual world. You can meet other people, watch a play, join in a game and even earn a living and a whole lot more. People do this for fun and in the hope of living their dream life.

I think people have enough trouble managing their lives in the real world and you can waste a huge amount of time in these virtual worlds, not really knowing what to do. It's probably best to focus on one small area to begin with so you can become familiar and gradually fine tune the things you want to do there.

And it's not just people doing this. Businesses recognise the massive number of people populating these virtual worlds and many are establishing their own presence there. Expect to see a lot of new forms of advertising.

Even governments are gearing up for the virtual world. Go to the Second Life website (http://secondlife.com/) and you will find virtual embassies for various countries where you can enter and meet with someone to get information about visas.

Businesses are finding other creative uses for virtual worlds. For example, where people are spread over a large area and need to get together to discuss things, they often organise a telephone conference. They all dial into a special number at a precise time and take it in turns to talk.

By setting up people with "avatars" in a virtual world website, they get to interact much more effectively and can "see" what's going on. Just like the real world, people may split into groups afterwards and maybe go and share a virtual cup of coffee in a virtual canteen to carry on the discussion. So the virtual world gives them a richer experience and is a perfect place for people to meet and collaborate.

Second Life even has its own currency, the Linden dollar, which can be exchanged for real money!

Young people are driving the growth of virtual worlds and there is some way to go before we see compelling reasons for everyone else to want to be in them. The technology still has some way to go so that, for example, you could create your own online virtual picture and reputation and take it with you to any of the many worlds, instead of having to have a separate one for each.

Virtual worlds work the computer very hard and require the maximum broadband connection to work well. If your computer is not up to scratch with a fast processor and plenty of memory or if you have a slow Internet connection, you will find the experience frustratingly slow and jerky and a lot of the pictures and graphics may be missing.

Discussion Forums

Want to connect with people with similar interests? Maybe you collect stamps, love golf or are a keen gardener. Wouldn't it be great to meet up with other people online to share, stories, information, tips etc.

The easiest way to do this is by using a "discussion forum".

Someone sets up a forum on a website and you go there just by entering the address in your browser. Normally, you need to register your name and email address and password so you can connect anytime you want and be identified to other participants in the forum when you write messages.

Think of it like a big message board. There will be a list of messages running down the board and each one of these shows just the title. This title is called a "thread". Usually, it will show the number of people who have read the message and the number who have typed in a response (referred to as posting a response).

So for example if you were looking at a forum about gardening, there may be a huge list of "threads" or titles for you to look at.

Where can I find a cheap greenhouse?

What' the best compost to use for roses?

The flower show was wonderful…

You look down the list of "threads" to read the titles until you find one that interests you. You click on it to read the first message and then any other messages that people have "posted" in response are shown in full below.

So, based on the example, you click on the message, "The flower show was wonderful". Then you can read this person's "post" in full. Plus if anyone else had anything to say about the show, his or her message would be underneath.

If you want, you can then add your own message "post" to the list of messages and everyone else can read it as well.

You can start your own "thread" discussion as well. Maybe you want to "post" a question and see if anyone can help you.

The number of discussion forums is endless. Everything from gardening, to dating to immigrating to house swaps to just about anything you can think of.

The best place to start is by using your search box and typing in:

"Discussion Forums" and then have a click around to find one you like.

Alternatively, companies like Google have discussion forums at http://www.googlecommunity.com.

Here's a list of threads in a Google sports forum:

Chapter 8 – Using the Internet 139

You can see someone posted a question: "Will David Beckham Play For England Again?" In the right hand column you can see that 276 people have read the question and 9 have posted replies. To see the replies and post your own, just click on the question title.

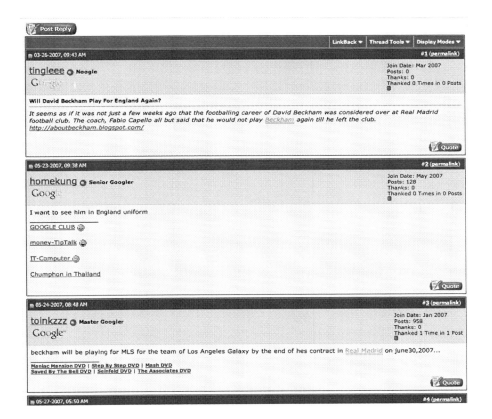

Blog

A blog is simply your personal "web log". If you want to rant and rave or encourage discussion about a hot topic, set up your soapbox with your personal blog on the Internet. You put up your thoughts and then anyone can come in and post a reply. You can choose to check and approve replies before they appear online if you want.

There is a special search engine website for blogs at www.technorati.com. Click on "Blogs" on the home page and you can browse blogs by topic to give you an idea of the wide variety there are and how they work.

If you are really serious about this, you might want to have a special web address for it (domain name). So this could be www.marysblogaboutglobalwarming.co.uk . Doing it this way though will cost money.

If you are happy with standard looking blog pages it's easy to use an automatic free service. The best known is www.blogger.com whilst others include www.wordpress.com and www.typepad.com.

It's not only individuals that have blogs. Many businesses do as well. They see it as a way to appear more "human" by posting messages and allowing the public to respond with theirs.

Spend some time searching for "blogs" to give you more ideas.

Dating

Dating websites are among the most popular on the Internet. You need to register your profile on a site to help others who are searching and then simply dive in and start meeting people. It goes without saying, since people are online you need to be aware that they may not always be who they appear to be and you should be certain and comfortable before you reveal your contact details or agree to meet.

There are dozens of sites to choose from and popular ones include www.datingdirect.com, www.match.com and www.datline.co.um

Chapter 8 – Using the Internet

There is even an online equivalent of speed dating at www.woome.com. You will need to register and have a web cam installed with your computer and you can wiz around tables meeting people in short sessions. The site is free, but if you meet someone you like and want their contact information it will cost you $1.

Millions of people have found old friends and even re-kindled old romances by using the website www.friendsreunited.com. It's free to look up people from your school or work days, but you have to pay to contact them.

A word of caution here though. I've heard stories of marriages and partnerships being split up when people have used this website to contact old loves from school days!

Your Own Domain

If having a blog isn't enough for you and you want to see your name up in Internet lights, then you can buy a web address (domain name) and create your own website.

For example, my personal website is www.markmeakings.com. There are many websites that will allow you to check availability and purchase online. Since practically every imaginable name will already be gone, you may need to be creative to get your name. For example, if www.jobloggs.com has gone, try getting www.jo-bloggs.com. Not as good, but not bad nonetheless. Alternatively the name ".com" may have gone, but the name ".co.uk" may be available.

Next you will need to buy a hosting account with an Internet Service Provider. This means buying space on one of their remote computers connected to the Internet. Quite often the same website that sells you the domain will also sell you the hosting. Enter "ISP" in your Internet search box to find them. Popular ones are www.uk2.net and www.easily.co.uk.

Lastly, you will need to create your website on your own computer. For this you will need a special program installed. Popular ones are Microsoft FrontPage for Windows PC's (www.microsoft.com) and Dreamweaver for the Apple Mac (www.adobe.com). You'll need quite a bit of spare time to learn and an evening class could be the ideal place to start.

Once you have "built" your website on your computer using one of these programs, you copy it (upload) over the Internet to the ISP's server computer (where you now have an account above). Your website can then be accessed by anyone over the Internet using your domain name, e.g. www.myname.com.

Video Websites.

Sites like www.youtube.com were first used by people uploading funny short videos for anyone to see. This is still the main use but such is the take up of this type of website that even businesses are using them to promote their products and services. There are literally millions of video clips on these video websites.

The View From Space

Google does just about everything. One neat free service is "Google Earth" (www.earth.google.com). It requires you to download some software for your Windows PC or Apple Mac. Then you can literally move around the planet from satellite images, go to places you have never seen before and even zoom in down to street level to see your own house! Go have a look at the Grand Canyon, Big Ben, the Sydney Harbour Bridge to name just a few.

Freephone

Referred to as VoIP (Voice Over Internet Protocol).

You can make phone calls from your computer over the Internet. It's free, easy and a lot of fun.

Here's how it works. You will need a microphone and speakers attached to your computer. Most new computers will have these built in, including many laptop computers. Alternatively, you can buy a special phone handset that plugs directly into your computer, so it really feels just like using a normal phone.

You sign up at a website that provides the phone service for free. The most well known is skype (www.skype.com) but there are plenty of others including Tesco (http://www.tescointernetphone.com/) and Demon (www.demon.net).

You can check out the Which? report to see the best for you at www.which.co.uk.

There are 2 types of call you can make. First you can call up someone who has also registered on the same free website and has set themselves up in the same way to make calls. This way you get to speak for free for as long as you want.

Chapter 8 – Using the Internet

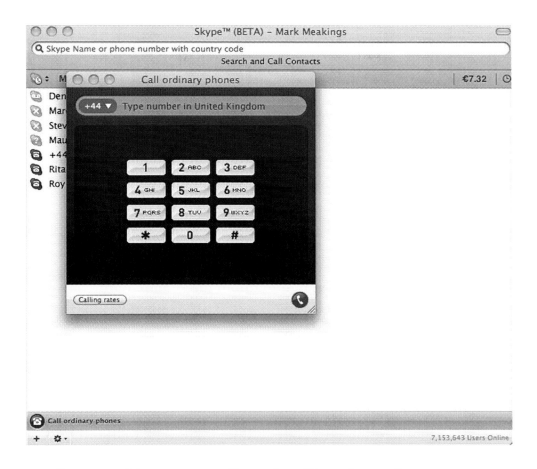

The second way enables you to call any landline phone from your computer. This is not free but very cheap. To use this service you buy a "top up" like a pay-as-you-go mobile phone. Using your credit card on the website, you can pay say £10. Then every time you call a landline, this amount is reduced until you need to top it up again.

Video Phone

This is identical to the free voice phone, however if you both have a web cam you can see each other as well as talk! A web cam is a tiny camera that connects to your computer that will show your face to the person on the other end of the line. Most computers nowadays will have a camera and microphone built in. If yours doesn't, you can pick one up from your local computer store.

With global warming such a crucial issue I'm always amazed more businesses don't use this instead of driving a hundred miles for a 60-minute meeting!

Give it a go, you'll love it!

Autopilot News And Information

RSS Feed. Don't worry about the acronym. Here's how it works. RSS saves you the trouble of visiting your favourite websites on a regular basis to see their latest news.

If the website offers RSS feed, you click on it and "subscribe" for free. Then whenever there is a change to that website a "news feed" is automatically sent to you.

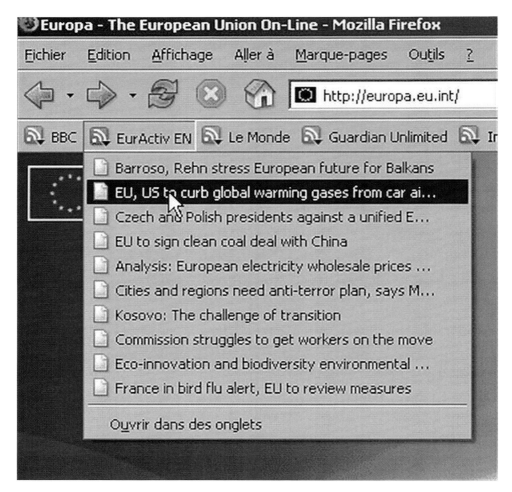

To receive this information feed, you need to have a program installed on your computer to handle this for you. There are plenty of free programs to download and install. Yahoo's RSS feed is very popular and has some great information and tips for you (http://news.yahoo.com/rss/)

Email On The Internet

Think of email like this. In order to send an email you must have an electronic address to send it to, just like a postal address on a letter. You must also have your own email address for people to send you an email.

If you are only going to use email for personal use with friends and family, you can use one of the free email websites on the Internet. Simply use your web browser program and go to one like www.googlemail.com and sign up for a free account.

Then every time you want to send or receive emails, you go to www.googlemail.com, sign in using your password and get going. Job done!

Chapter 8 – Using the Internet

The advantage of using **Internet** Email is that it is free to use and you can access it from any computer with an Internet connection. This is great if you are travelling, or maybe using an Internet Café or if you are using someone else's computer and just want to check your email.

The disadvantage is your screen will be covered in adverts from the email websites you are using to send your messages. This helps them cover the cost of the free service.

Also you cannot always choose a suitable email address e.g. john.brown@googlemail.com as there is probably someone else already using it. So you often compromise with something like john.brown99@googlemail.com. Also, using Googlemail or any of the other free ones tells people you are using a free account and this is not the best image for a business.

When you use free Internet email, your message emails are stored on the website you are using and not on your computer.

I use these free email accounts for throwaway use. Sometimes in order to get access to a website you have to give your email address. They keep your email address (and even sell it on) to people who will send you unsolicited emails (called SPAM email). This can be very annoying.

So you start to notice you are receiving emails from people and companies you've never heard of trying to sell you stuff you don't want. That would be OK if it were just a few, but to give you an idea of how it can get out of control, I sometimes have 300 spam emails on a Monday morning! Apart from the waste of my time sorting and deleting them (some email programs will do this for you automatically), quite often they are offensive.

When you send an email, you type up your message and you can add an attachment to it. For example, you could email a friend and attach a photo with it. Some of the spam emails come with an attachment file but they can be fatal if you open them up to look at them as they can install a virus onto your computer without you knowing.

This is where a virus protection program will help you as it will scan these for you to ensure they are safe but spam email is still very risky.

So, if you use a free Internet email account, when this gets too much just close it down and open a new one with a new address and start again. For example, close down john.brown99@googlemail.com and open up a new account like john.brown101@googlemail.com

So get yourself a free email account and start using it straightaway.

Typical Internet Email

As you can see, you use your Internet browser program to go to the free Internet email website (in this case, Google's email website). You can choose to check for new email, compose a new email and print your email. Have a look at a few of the free email sites and decide which one you like best. You will have to register your details with them and they will give you an email address that you give to other people so they can write to you.

Typical ISP Email

I also use my Internet Service Providers specialist email service for business and for family and friends as well. I guard this email address and only give it to people I know and trust. I don't want this to be "spammed" with rubbish email, as I don't want to have to close it down and lose my special email address. Using this email service, my emails are stored on my computer as opposed to being kept on some distant computer owned by a free web-based email service provider.

The difference with this email is that you pay for it, but you are more likely to get the email address you want (e.g. paul.bates@bt.com.). You will normally pay for it when you sign up for Internet access with your Internet Service Provider like BT, OneTel, Sky etc.

Chapter 8 – Using the Internet

Plus you will use a special email program to send and receive email (not your Internet browser program). This has no adverts and is faster and more flexible to use.

This email program usually comes with your computer. On a Windows PC it is normally Microsoft "Outlook" or "Outlook Express". Outlook Express deals with email, but Outlook also has a personal calendar built in as well.

On an Apple Mac it is simply called "Mail". There is a separate calendar program that comes with the computer called "iCal".

These programs are often called "email clients".

When you use your Internet Service Providers email, this is separate from the "normal" Internet where you go to look at websites. They will have separate computers (email servers) that just send, receive and store email messages. You will have your own personal mailbox and email address to use e.g. obloggs@bt.com.

Your ISP will provide you with details of their email computer that you access over the phone line, together with your email address, password and other information.

You start your email program (normally Outlook or Mail) and first off you need to set up an "email account" in the program. This simply means you enter the information the ISP gave you. Then next time you start the program, it will automatically connect to the ISP's email computer over the telephone line.

Windows Outlook Mail Program

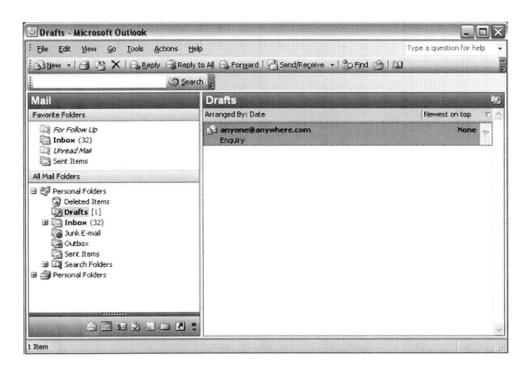

Apple Mac's Mail Program

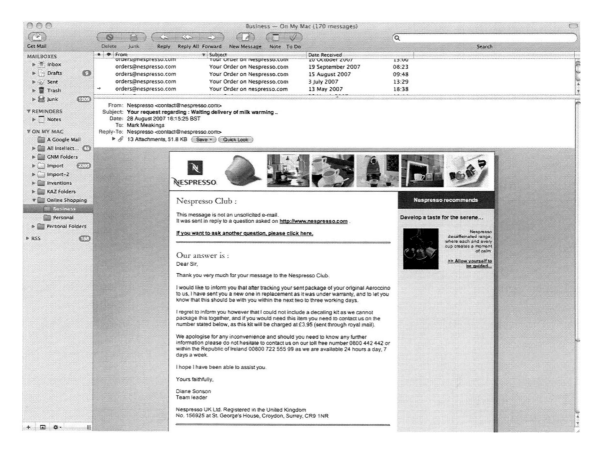

People sending emails to your email address, will have their messages stored on your ISP's special email computer. When you connect to the same computer, the email messages are automatically downloaded into your email program where they can be read, printed, stored, passed on, replied to etc.

You may get a lot of email over time and there's no reason not to keep it on your computer if you have a reasonable size hard disk. I have email on mine over 12 years totalling over 50,000 messages! With a simple search though, I can go back and check any of those messages.

With so much email, it's vital to organise it BEFORE it gets too much. I talked about creating folders on your hard disk at the start. You need to do the same thing now, but within your email program. You will find a function to create a new folder. Set up folders for all the types of messages you will have. E.g. business, family, finance, legal, etc. You can add, delete or amend them as you go along over time.

All new messages automatically go into the "inbox". If you want to keep one, simply click and drag it to the folder you created earlier.

This makes filing and finding email easy and it keeps your inbox to a reasonable size.

You will find plenty of email tips in the KAZ "Master Your Day" book available to download free at www.kaz-type.com/freedownloads.asp

Conclusion

My aim with this book is to give you the basics of personal computing so that you may be confident in choosing, using and getting the best from them.

I hope you can now see that learning about computers is not difficult. All it takes is some basic knowledge, a little bit of courage and determination.

There is only so much that I can cover in this book and I know there may well be more you want to learn about.

I am preparing a host of short accelerated learning products for you that will take you step by step further into using your computer. Go to my website, www.computertrainingexpert.co.uk, for full details.

While you are at my website, you will also be able to check out any new free downloads to help you.

Since I know I won't have answered all your questions in this book, you will also be able to let me know your most burning questions about computers. I will do my best to cover it for you either at my website, on my free email newsletter or in the next update of this book.

Appendix Of Computer Terms

There are hundreds of terms that refer to everything to do with computers. I have mentioned many in this book alongside the everyday meaning.

The most comprehensive library of terms I have found has been created at www.webopedia.com. I suggest you create a bookmark with your web browser program (see earlier section) so that you can refer to them if necessary.

Keyboard Shortcuts

An alternative to using the mouse is to use a combination of keys to achieve the same results. Some people find this quicker once they have remembered them. If you go to my website and download your free bonus e-book "Master Your Day" you will find I have listed some of the most useful there for you plus 89 other ways to make the most of your time and computer. You will find it at www.markmeakings.com .